Praise for

Recovered Essence:

How Toxic Relationships
Impact Your Inner Child

Christine states in her book, Recovered Essence: "Your past pain becomes a gift from God to others." Her story, with corresponding scripture and teaching is truly going to be a gift to anyone who has walked the difficult road to abuse. Those who read it will glean Godly wisdom, guidance and hope. As a Pastor, I will be recommending this truth-filled book as an aid to those needing emotional healing.

—Lynne Biddle
Care Pastor, Christian Celebration Center

"It is with great pleasure that I read Christine's autobiography "Recovered Essence: How Toxic Relationships Impact Your Inner Child" I had the pleasure to know Christine and her ex-husband during the duration of their turbulent marriage and can vouch first hand of the extreme difficulty Christine and her daughters endured.

I am so proud of this work that so well depicts the pain, shame, and struggle that she endured yet chose to guard her heart from offense and bitterness in the midst of unthinkable betrayal. Unfortunately life is not always fair and striving to do what is right is not easy. This book will help many others who find themselves victims of the choices of significant others in their lives as they relate to Christine as she pours out her heart with such honestly and transparency.

I am confident that regardless of what life throws at you, it is possible to be victorious and faithful to God. This story will help if you find yourself overcome by heartache and betrayal and will point you to where there is true hope.

Well done Christine."

—Pastor Cathy Ciaramitaro
Co-pastor of Windsor Christian Fellowship
Author, *The Cross: The Power The Purpose The Passion,*
How to Change Your Hell into Heaven
Executive Director of Windsor Life Centre –
(a women's Rehab Centre)

Recovered Essence:
How Toxic Relationships
Impact Your Inner Child

by Christine A. Wilson

ISBN 978-0-692-02758-5

Published by

Wilson Wellness Counseling, Coaching and Consulting LLC

christineawilson.com
Boyne City, Michigan
49712

Contact Christine at:
christine@recoveredessence.com
info@wilsonwellnesscounseling.com

In Association with
köehlerstudios™

Disclaimer: All scripture is referenced from the Holy Bible and the translated versions of the scriptures used are shortened into acronyms.

The events written in this book, *Recovered Essence: How Toxic Relationships Impact Your Inner Child*, is my recollection of events to the best of my knowledge. Some identities have been changed. I have no intention to hurt anyone, or cause division amongst family members. I regret any unintentional harm resulting from the public marketing of this book. My only aim is to offer hope for those who are hurting.

This book is not intended as a substitute for the advice of a therapist.
Although the author and publisher have made every effort to ensure that the information in this book was correct at press time, the author and publisher do not assume and hereby disclaim any liability to any party for any loss, damage, or disruption caused by errors or omissions, whether such errors or omissions result from negligence, accident, or any other cause.

Recovered Essence

How Toxic Relationships Impact Your Inner Child

Christine A. Wilson

Dedications

To my two beautiful daughters, Natasha and Jericka:

You are my most precious gifts given to me by God. Over the years, I wondered how you would endure, but honestly, I'm amazed and proud of you both. In every area you suffered from your childhood; I pray that you discover the greater measure of His faithfulness, peace and love.

Malcolm: You are my knight in shining armor I've longed for all my life. After all my struggles, your love and support brought resolution to this story. The words in our song, "When God Made You," are so perfect: "Gone are all the questions about why, and I've never been so sure of anything in my life." Words cannot express how thankful I am to be your wife.

To my clients and coworkers who became friends over the years: I'm thankful for all your love and understanding. I'm glad that the field of cosmetology brought us together.

Thanks to our families at Windsor Christian Fellowship and Christian Celebration Center who loved my daughters and me through difficult times.

To my Abba Father and Lord Jesus Christ, who revealed your unwavering love for me, even at times when I was least worthy; You saw the pain and knew why I was weak. Thank you for the strength to revisit these memories and may the words in this book accomplish that which you desire in each soul: to be grounded in Your love.

"When Christ dwells in your heart through faith, you are grounded in love and able to comprehend His love which passes knowledge and be filled with God's goodness."

Ephesians 3:17-19 NKJV (Paraphrased)

Table of Contents

Preface

TO FEEL CONNECTED and belong is a basic human need. Unfortunately, many of us enter a relationship before adequately knowing and loving ourselves, let alone another person. The quality of our relationships usually reflects how we see ourselves internally. Emotional intimacy involves a deeper trust, allowing someone to discover the true essence of a person. If we enter a relationship prematurely, we may miss how they handle life's pressures. The trigger of an internal conflict is where many problems begin in relationships and is also the birthplace of toxicity.

Wounded people are often attracted to other wounded people. Understanding the effects of wounds from the past can help foster relationships to work effectively. This will take a deeper connection, not just a surface relationship. It involves not just the minds and bodies of both people but also their inner core essences. If you are not living life through your true essence, not only is there conflict in your relationship, but within yourself. Allow me to explain:

Our hearts are often thought of as our essence, spirit or core. Time, physical age, appearance and possessions have little to do with our inner essence. Our essence is the part of our being where *perfect love* can function in and through us. It matures differently than our physical being and our mind. Our spirit, our essence or core is connected to our destiny and eternity. It operates by divine love and understands *the truth,* not *our own temporary and changing truth.* Our sensual truth is relative to our own surrounding influences, childhood experiences and possibly wounded souls. Divine truth gives us a healthy model for our deepest essence to be recovered. Only then can the sacredness of pure love in our relationships be experienced. This is much different than Hollywood and romance novels often portray love. It goes much deeper because we are multidimensional beings.

Deep down we know the difference between whole and wounded, wrong and right. We were created with this law in our hearts. (See Romans 2:15.) Our soul manages our mind and emotions based on our own beliefs, experiences and perceptions. We are more conscious of what our soul tells us yet our soul is still affected by our essence. Sometimes it's a *knowing* or *leading* we experience when our heart is telling us something. We should be willing to learn more about what our essence is yearning for before entering a relationship.

Toxicity in relationships is usually rooted in childhood, so it helps to consider its impact on our soul. Our true essence began to form in those family systems. No family functioned perfectly. Parents may have been unaware of their child's internal conflict. Secrets and silent fears buried inside the mind of a child may not erupt until years later. If there was a lack of the necessary bonding and nurturing, or trust had been violated early in life, certain hormones and neurotransmitters, which aid in the brain's processing of events, can be hampered during puberty. Instead, adrenaline overrides these chemical functions, giving way for the natural instinct for survival. The *fight or flight* response becomes more necessary than becoming vulnerable or negotiable. The child within cannot sort out the confusion, especially without communication, so the core of that person freezes in its ideal emotional development. Science calls this *arrested development* or *fixation.*

The essence of a person can only grow as the will and understanding permits. In the way a child guards what is meaningful to them; they will subconsciously guard that which was lost in innocence—safety and control. Their soul *survives* through life in conflict with their true essence, resulting in a lost identity.

Their ego operates as a substitute identity to fit in, hiding who they really are at their core. When conflict arises in their personal relationships, they may try therapy and adapt to methods, change communication or break a habit which doesn't always help the child, still wounded inside. A side note: Throughout this book, I will use the terms; *frozen* or *arrested* development, *ego*, *identity* and a *pseudo personality*, all interchangeably.

Some victims of trauma have succeeded outwardly, burying the core issues so deeply in denial, expressed many years later through abuse, behavior disorders or addictions. They may act one way at work, yet abusive at home because a deeper level of closeness requires a trust they've never learned. Since the brain stopped normal development, they are immature in their more intimate emotional relationships with their spouses, kids and other family members. Emotionally, they may act as a child because they never developed the skills to manage emotions through a healthy maturing process. As an adult, their alternative identity or ego attempts to maintain control of a delicate situation bound for further dismay. Sadly, when a concerned person tries to address the behavior, or share their need for emotional connection, they may react in anger or denial, and project blame or become cunningly deceptive. They avoid feeling vulnerable and powerless again, making emotional intimacy more difficult. Their toxic behavior is not the true person but the identity that guards the wounded child within. Sadly, as a result, people end up in prison, some are suicidal, and some develop a mental disorder. They lost touch with their true essence and the potential meaningful relationships.

Addictive behavior, abuse and co-dependency are functioning coping patterns formed from earlier experiences. These compulsive and repetitive cycles prevent deeper fulfillment in relationships. They limit emotional maturing of all who are involved. It is essential for those cycles to be broken in order for deeper emotional bonding and to bring our essence back to life.

We are spiritual beings with human tendencies therefore our brains do reflect our spirituality whether a person believes it or not. God made the brain with the ability to re-define those old memories which may have arrested the emotional development in childhood. A relationship that promotes emotional bonding through trust, accountability and respect, over time can take the place of unhealthy patterns. The neurotransmitters in the brain can literally be redirected by the power of the will to accept perfect love, truth and wise counsel. A new reality of safety, trust and unconditional love can even reduce unhealthy genealogical tendencies. The damaged child can heal and connect again to their essence in a new trusted system. People begin to understand what *a healthy normal* feels like. Anyone who has experienced freedom from emotional captivity at this level knows that this is well with their soul. I am one of them. We are not just survivors, but overcomers.

> *"For everyone has been born of God overcomes the world. And this is the victory that overcomes the world—our faith."*
> *1 John 5:4 ESV*

If a failed relationship has brought you to the point of change in your life, this book gets into the finer details of what makes us really tick, what are the real obstacles and what fulfils us at our core. Many people know they have a problem but don't know how to fix it. Sadly, many therapists don't know either. I'm privileged to have been on both ends of this great challenge. I've experienced the confusion, desperation, the solution and the freedom to living through my essence.

Over the years I've explored the realms affecting the total person. The trending research in emotional intelligence and neuro-linguistic programming have been helpful as it involves relational connection. A person"s Intelligence Quotient is different than their Emotional Quotient. In the future we will be hearing more about a person's Spiritual Quotient as we are multidimensional beings. I'm optimistic that the connections of neuroscience, spirituality, physics and psychology uniting this testimony will be a shortcut to clearer answers for you and your loved ones. My prayer is that it leads you on the path to a love that sets your essence free within the earthen vessel of your being.

> *"For God hath not given us the spirit of fear, but of power and of love and a sound mind."*
> *2 Timothy 1:7 KJV.*

Prologue

IN CONVERSATIONS WITH people, if I talk about my past, I'm often asked: "How did you get through it all? You seem quite normal!"

I will never forget where I came from. It keeps me passionate about my message. Being a deep thinker who enjoys connecting with people, I gathered my personal thoughts and independent research that accompany my story. This will likely be a different kind of reading experience for you. I don't like wasting people's time with *rambling* unless it's part of a bigger and necessary point. I was sure to use relevant, evidence-based, most effective and/or useful concepts from every sphere of influence affecting our lives. It might help bring clarity to the fog of information out there today, particularly for those who may relate to my story.

A story creates a safe place to meet someone. While reading it, you can unmask and be real while we share some realities about ourselves. Owning the mistakes of our past can make us more powerful. This helps us value what was learned, make a connection and unite with a passion to help others. Embracing our pain connects our humanity.

I agonized over how to communicate everything I had in my heart to write. Studies have shown that the metaphoric influence of a story connects with people and that's my goal.

So I decided to blend two books in one, as a self-help/memoir. Each chapter concludes with relevant key points consisting of scientific, spiritual and/or psychological reflection, relating to that chapter's phase of life and development. Similar to a therapist bringing a patient back through their past, this helps to recognize how our beliefs formed our thoughts and subsequently our choices. I will bring you alongside the timeline of my story to show how managing life from our deepest essence allows the purity of grace to restore and develop us. As the story unfolds, the insights reveal why our dreams may fail and our essence can become lost. The story sections are written in the mindset, perception and insight which I had at that time. My lack of direction and limited insight as I grew through the years is transparent and humbling, but the truth. Taking a shortcut to our Promised Land can actually keep us from it.

> *"I will instruct you and teach you in the way you should go: I*
> *will counsel you with my eye upon you."*
> *Psalm 32:8 ISV*

Pursuing my own happy family was a goal since childhood. Along that quest, I discovered a love that held they key for true happiness; a personal relationship with God through our Savior, Jesus Christ. I thought I'd gained the wisdom needed to see my dreams realized. I would recreate my painful past into a perfect family of my own. Because of earlier maladaptive thought patterns and beliefs about myself, others and God, it was easy to get off the straight and narrow path. The truth must get tested through adversity to bring about the fullness of our essence.

My dream became reality, but soon so did my nightmare. Through times of despair I was forced to relinquish my control just to survive. The more I surrendered my control, letting God have more control, the stronger I became, gaining healthy control where I lacked it. It was much harder than it sounds; in fact it was agonizing. It took many years to learn where I end and God begins. I'm not alone. We all have to work with the map we've been given. I'm hoping to shorten your journey to your Promised Land and live fully engaged within your Recovered Essence.

A side note; toward the end of the story, the last piece of the puzzle of my life comes together and everything makes sense. Please be sure to read through carefully and not miss out on the best part.

I ask you not to pass judgment on the choices made by anyone in this book. I agonized over certain pieces, but chose to focus on the souls who need to know that someone on this earth knows their pain. Most of us in this book were victims of less fortunate and painful childhoods. Hurting-people can hurt people. In exposing the dynamics of these events, my only motive is to encourage those in toxic relationships and those who want to understand their pain, to find their voice and path to complete healing. If you allow your heart to be open throughout my story, maybe something will resonate with yours or someone else's life you care about. My prayer is that you find more meaning for your life and peace for your heart as you read.

"And we know that God causes all things to work together for good for those who love God, to those who are called according to His purpose."

Romans 8:28 NASB

Introduction

WE WERE CREATED to experience intimate connections and belong. Why were some of us drawn to people that may eventually hurt us? Could there have been an underlying attraction overlooked in the beginning? Did our dreams for a happy future develop out of fear and lack of love? Overcoming the toxic relationship may require examining what got us there in first place. Our relationships have something to teach us about our emotional self, our true essence and the incomplete child within.

Dysfunctional relationships are built on shaky foundations and by incomplete people. The poor choices of our ancestors which were left unredeemed continue to plague us with a propensity for familiar vices. Through much of our lives we operate from mental maps created from childhood that are difficult to redesign. It takes conscious effort and strong beliefs to re-map our thoughts, memories and maladaptive beliefs. It is necessary to examine our framework before looking at the problems in a present relationship. The first few chapters will provide such a platform. Regardless of our age, it is important to consider the child within. We all still have some growing up to do, but will our adult ego cooperate with a higher and more trustworthy authority? Are we teachable?

God has a plan for us that's better than the one we have for ourselves. The quality of our relationships may verify this. Unsuccessful connections should challenge us to explore our emotional and spiritual lives. Some of us communicate love in counterproductive ways because we don't realize how valuable we are to God or why we became alienated from Him. Throughout this book, I reference this stage as our *orphaned essence*, when we have not known the love we were made to experience. An intimate knowledge of God's redeeming love helps us to gain a more effective model of how to love others wisely. At the phase when we accept His love in our hearts and become willing to get Him involved, we become His *adopted children.*

Like any other meaningful relationship, you'll have to spend some time getting to know His true character and the dynamics of this relationship. He is our perfect loving parent and best friend beyond that which we've ever known. The type of trust required with God is deeper than human trust and likewise the outcome. It's much more personal and intimate because it's spiritual and not intuitive. It involves a unique exchange which is crucial to understand. Christians who don't understand the roles of the Holy Spirit and grace often get off course because many don't reach the point of abandon and trust. The contrary is that we learn to let His Spirit carry the burdens of what we cannot control so God can build our strength where we are weak. We cannot learn this love on our own because "that which is born of the flesh is flesh and that which is born of the Spirit is spirit" (John 3:6 ESV). This higher love must be received in true faith, experienced and expressed within our essence by the Holy Spirit whom God sent to us.

> *"And I will ask the Father and He will give you another helper to be with you forever, even the spirit of truth whom the world cannot receive because it neither sees him nor knows him. You know him for he dwells in you and will be with you. I will not leave you as orphans; I will come to you."*
>
> *John 14:16-18 ESV*

This exchange of control can only come through surrender and faith in His love, then grace can take over the burden that is not ours to carry. This process requires authentic spiritual intimacy, which I will illustrate in the following pages. His words contain truth, power and authority and can activate His promises in your life. These are the gifts and inheritance which belong to us as His kids. Anyone who believes and trusts in them will gain wisdom, healing, strength and fulfillment through grace, the power of God's Holy Spirit working with us. Watch God *foster* your heart and life as you trust Him in faith in your *adopted* essence. These truths personify the Laws of Attraction and Quantum Mechanics, going beyond physics into the powerful relationship with God Himself. This emotionally intimate relationship will help define the deeper part of you, your spirit, wherein lies your *recovering* essence, your true self.

"Looking unto Jesus, the Author and the Finisher of our faith."
Hebrews 12:2 KJV

Chapter 1

Family: Love's First Imprint

BOTH OF MY parents grew up in Windsor, Ontario, Canada. When I was six years old and my sister Yvette was four, we all moved to the small town of Ruthven, about one hour from Windsor. Life in the country would be a new experience for all of us. It was a large property with 3 barns and a large fenced pasture. My mom left her job at General Motors to stay and work at home on the farm, and my dad commuted to Windsor daily to work at Chrysler. Both parents worked hard.

My dad would often come home from the Comber Farm Auctions with animals. I had the privilege of helping to raise at least two of every kind of farm animal imaginable. There were about fifteen cats around the property; some tame and others wild. I fell in love with the animals, and sadly, some were being raised to later eat for dinner. I remember helping my dad kill the chickens. I was told to hold the twine roped around a chicken's neck as he held its feet in one hand and an ax in the other. It was quite funny watching them run around without a head!

I had the experience of milking goats and cows, collecting eggs and watched a baby calf being born. I spent much time with our horses and I loved to ride. We had newborn goats and many baby chicks, ducks and geese roaming the property. We had guard geese which we had to outrun to get from one place to the other or they would attack, unless I stopped the most aggressive one by holding him by his neck until whomever I was protecting got by.

I loved the adventures of climbing trees, building forts, catching critters and playing with the kids next door. We had so many places to explore on our farms. Life was so much fun with endless things to do, play with, and imagine. I was a bit of a daring show-off, which sometimes got me injured or in trouble, but thrills were so exciting. If others could do it, then I could too.

There was a mysterious peace in the nature and simplicity around me. I felt it while lying in a hay loft, watching a mother cat with her kittens as I dreamed about life in the future.

My mom and dad taught us much about the workings of inside and outside the house. Dad always had many projects on the go and plans to unfold. We learned what it was like to work hard, but we had the benefits of this wonderful experience on a farm. It was fun sharing our home with cousins and friends when they came to visit..

I remember when we were very young, Yvette and I would dress in our ballerina-style slips and perform dances in hopes to impress our audience. On my toy piano I played simple songs by ear and imagined being a talented musician.

I loved gymnastics and even without extra lessons, I managed to learn from those who did have them. I was determined to stand out, so I always gave it my very best in every area of life. As an over-achiever, I wanted to learn everything I could so I could stay ahead of the game and be worth noticing.

I was quite inquisitive about life and preferred accurate and true answers. I wanted to know more about the unclear side of life and asked many questions that were probably hard for my parents to answer. I was intrigued by the mysteries of heaven and earth and drawn to the unseen as if I somehow had access to it. I wanted to be a part of something bigger than the world around me. Otherwise I was a very typical country girl.

Life seemed for the most part average, although there was little positive affirmation and more criticism from my dad. He liked to see us learn things that he had interest in or where we could be of assistance. When that didn't work out the way he hoped, he would at times get frustrated with us. His irritation was quite obvious and discipline was very painful with the belt on our bottoms.

We didn't have grandparents who could make up for any need of affirmation and love. My mom's mother died at age forty-five and my dad's mom had Alzheimer's disease so I don't ever remember her in her healthy mind. Neither of my grandfathers were the loving, praising or affectionate types.

Mom and Dad argued once in a while and I hated when they did. There was one argument that seemed especially bad. As I listened to the fight, I stared outside at the seemingly angry wind blowing the trees; I began to fear that something bad would soon happen to our family. The future was unknown, just as mysterious as the wind, like a force of its own, threatening to interrupt our life as we knew it. I understood that God was very big and all-knowing but I began to question: *God, why is this happening to my family?*

My mom did teach us to pray to God and ask Him for help. He was up there somewhere in heaven, and I basically thought of Him as good and maybe someone to fear if He was mad. I never blamed Him for bad things that happened because there was a devil in this world but not in heaven. I may have questioned like most people; why couldn't God stop bad things from happening? As a baby I was baptized in the Catholic Church, but we didn't regularly attend Mass, and my knowledge of God was quite limited. I could pray to Him, but I didn't see things change. There were more prevalent messages I began to learn about life.

When I was eleven years old my parents separated and my mom left the home. I was devastated and felt torn in half, wishing somehow I could stay with both parents. I would have done anything to prevent that happening and offered everything I could to show my mom what it meant to me if she would stay. But I couldn't change my mom's mind. She had some friends that gave her the courage to be strong enough to not put up with things any longer. I wasn't sure what she was leaving for and don't recall any explanation. When I had to choose where to go, I could stay in the current family home and the familiar settings with my father and the farm animals, or move to Kingsville and live with my sister and my mother in a small upstairs apartment downtown.

The problem about going with my mom was that she had a new male friend, who I really didn't want around, especially when he seemed to be overly affectionate with my mom. Maybe he was the reason she left my dad.

I had witnessed this man's brother chasing my dad with a large knife and fighting on the ground with him. Some other people came to stop their fight as my mom and another woman were screaming. I was horrified but as I saw my dad get up and come over to where his motorcycle was on the ground, he was not badly hurt. He looked at me with tears in his eyes as he rode away.

I tried everything to get my parents back together. For the first couple of weeks I stayed at home with my dad. One day at school, I was called to the principal's office and I saw my mom sitting there. She spoke to the principal and she took me home with her. I remember questioning the principal if this was right and he simply responded, "She's your mother and therefore there's nothing I can do."

A couple of days later at my mom's apartment, disappointed with her "new friend" being over, I was crying and looking out the window at the angry wind blowing the trees again. It reminded me of that same familiar sadness and fear of the future, questioning God about my family and life. My dad suddenly appeared through the bushes in the darkness below. He spoke quietly: *Chris! Come back home on the bus!*

I did not sleep at all that night, being so confused about what to do. The next day after school, I did what my dad said and I came home by bus to stay on the farm with my dad and the animals. By returning home, this also communicated my anger to my mom for leaving and having a man around. I felt so sorry for my father since I saw him cry during this period.

I decided to stay with him and I accepted the role of the housewife—cooking, cleaning, and taking care of the farm animals. I knew my hard work cheered my dad up and made him value me more. It was kind of like playing house. I felt like I was growing up so quickly for an eleven-year-old. It was like I replaced my mom's presence. I became angrier at my mom for choosing to break up our home and showing more attention to another man, other than my dad.

One day, my dad gave me the birds and bees talk and showed me books with naked people in them. He understood that I didn't like my mom's new boyfriend around her. He explained how he knew that I wouldn't want a new lady in the house to replace my mom either. He enlightened to me that dads have a need to feel things with a woman and that I could help him with this. He wasn't forceful at all, besides, he arose my curiosity with those books. I learned some things that I was sure no other girls my age knew about. It was strange in a way, but he was my dad; I trusted him and this was our special little secret. I valued and craved his affectionate and more-approving side.

Eventually a pretty lady named Shirley started hanging around a lot and I was troubled when they were in his bedroom alone. I think she didn't like me either. She got mad at me one time when I was telling on her two-year-old daughter when she was bad. Shirley didn't last very long around our house. Shortly after, another very pretty lady named Liz, who was a model, became dad's new girlfriend and even moved in with us but their relationship didn't last long either.

Throughout the next few years my dad struggled to find and keep a woman to replace my mom's presence in our home. I always tried to be nice especially if his girlfriends were nice to me. Unfortunately there were quite a few that came into our lives but they each left after a short period of time.

Eventually, the way to normalize life was doing whatever I possibly could for my dad to keep him from feeling frustrated and overwhelmed with the workload or issues he had. I also feared him when he was frustrated or angry. I grew to work excessively hard and give of myself to avoid any negative outbursts. I don't recall being asked how I felt or what I thought.

At school and with friends I tried to portray myself as though nothing was wrong with my life. I did my best to fit in, but I often felt that others had everything better. I often wore clothes from the Goodwill Store and did without the fancier extras which the other kids had. I was embarrassed to have friends over because my dad began to salvage things and started piles of metal, tires and other scrap. Many unfinished projects made our home and property looked cluttered.

I remember feelings of turmoil and sadness but there was

no outlet in which I could sort out or understand all that was happening in my life. I wanted to be liked by my friends and by my teacher, Mrs. Gubinsky. One day I'd missed her instructions not to use my eraser on my paper. She came over and grabbed my hair and shook my head back and forth, yelling angry words at me. My mind was elsewhere that day. I remember feeling alone and very sad. There was no one else in my life that could help me like a parent, teacher or grandparent who might ask me questions about my feelings or what was happening in my life.

"Give sorrow word; the grief that does not speak knits up the o-er wrought heart and bids it break."
William Shakespeare

Family: Loves First Imprint
Key Points

"Jesus said, Let the little children come to me, and do not hinder them for the kingdom of heaven belongs to such as these."
Matthew 19:14 NIV

Our Essence is Secure in Love

THE FIRST PLATFORM of love is our family; a safe place of security, training and love. In the family unit we are meant to learn how to trust, obey and bond in relationships. Before leaving home we should have been safely trained for life and how to properly give and receive love. The way we sought value in the home will be a framework for our future relationships.

Children crave love, validation and structure from both parents. An unavailable parent creates a void in a child's heart, sometimes leading children to unpleasant behavior for mere attention or a need to be understood. The broken family can cause a deeper sense of alienation, weakening the foundation where the pure essence of a child grows. Children feel secure when their unique efforts, thoughts, interests and feelings are acknowledged by both parents. A child's perception of their value will affect the development of their true identity and quality of their future relationships.

A father is one of the most influential models in a girl's life. From infant to teen, his impact will affect her confidence, self-image and her role as a woman in relationship to a man. A dad in a girl's life is seen as her first love. She may seek a love similar to his style emotionally and/or externally.

A dad in a boy's life is to be his first hero and is the model for manhood. The father's persona imparts the child's interpretation of protection, provision, justice and strength. Dads were meant to deliver encouraging directives worthy of reverence, respect and accountability. Moms more commonly provide nurture and love. Together, both parents equally bond with the child to help them feel safe and securely prepared for adult life. These foundational principles also support spiritual laws which also aid in the maturity of their spiritual essence and their relationship as a child of God. The divinely tailored roles of discipline plus love develops an emotionally healthy person. This sets the emotional foundation for a trusting authority in their lives, thus making them better equipped to operate in the fullness of their essence. In fact, Jesus was the perfect model, as He personified love in both humanity and deity along with His obedience to God.

Many of us were overly dominated; we became fearful and lost trust. We were left alone, emotionally abandoned, without the emotional connection responsible for guiding our true essence. Many of our spirits were broken. Fear replaced trust in authority. We came out of an era when we were literally taught not to talk or feel. Our true essence could not grow as it should, since our foundation is laced with fear. There was little support and education available to victims of abuse compared to today. Without support our essence trusted in superficial means to cope. The result: an *orphaned essence.*

Mothers today seem to have more input in parenting styles since finding their voice after the women's movement. Our present generation of millennials is more in touch with the motherly influence of love. The pendulum has swung so far that the fathers' role as a trusted and respectful leader in the home was minimized because mothers would not tolerate aggressive dominance and rightly so. Therefore, on the downside, without a father's loving discipline and teaching, many millennials lack respect for authority, moral and spiritual directives. The culture today is more self-centered, less self-disciplined and lacks conviction about what is noble, upright and sustainable. They need good fathers who are strong and trusted leaders in their lives to develop tangible virtues of courage, leadership and masculinity. Without that relationship, they cannot fully grasp what they have lacked.

The fallout of the imbalanced and broken family has a ripple effect on our culture today, veering further away from Gods design, the perfect balance of mother and father, love and truth. Obedience is attained out of love and not fear. This is the best foundation by which our essence can develop perfectly. With the great challenges today, our children need the pendulum in the middle again, just as the clearly instructed roles in the bible. See Colossians 3:18-21

The Need to Communicate Feelings

"Speak up for those who cannot speak for themselves, for the rights of all who are destitute."
Proverbs 31:8 NIV

All emotions are valid and real and worth questioning. Parents should have enough empathy, skill and sensitivity to assist a child to work through them. That responsibility involves helping their children to identify their negative feelings, to communicate them and develop healthy coping strategies to manage them. This allows the inner frustrations to have an outlet, instead of acting out negatively. Parents who have not quite managed their own emotions will likely not be very effective in teaching their children in this way. Instead, many parents allow their children to dictate their responses. Parents need to go deeper, yet many live on the surface today.

When children learn to feel, think and act freely within healthy boundaries, their true identity has a better chance to blossom. Emotional learning helps young children be in touch with their feelings, which allows their talents, personalities and social skills to advance beyond their age. Communicating feelings constructively is one of the most important relational necessities of today. They will use this skill the rest of their lives. Many adults are emotionally less mature than some children because they were never taught the skills to identify, communicate and control their emotions in childhood. Harsh discipline in their own childhood may have broken their spirit, or in other words, frozen their emotional development.

"Train up a child in the way he should go; even when he is old
he will not depart from it."
Proverbs 22:6 ESV

The Unconscious Search for Emotional Survival

Emotions connect and disconnect us. Fearful memories are difficult to erase. They are stored in the amygdala, which is the integrative center of the brain where emotional behavior has its roots. If a child's imprint of love was tainted with rejection, physical, emotional or sexual abuse before adolescence, that memory stored in the amygdala causes an interruption of the normal development in the brain. The excess adrenaline provides a mode of protection for survival for that child, since trust was violated. This is called the *fight or flight response.* When a child has experienced this, the threat remains in the amygdala and they adapt to methods that *seemed* to work in their family dynamics. The neurotransmitters in the brain begin to build connections that map out how they will survive in the future, subconsciously operating in a mode of self-protection. Relationships become adjusted and molded into those familiar patterns that for years worked to keep them in control. The underdeveloped essence remains emotionally alienated yet perceivably *safe.* The quality of true intimacy and emotional maturity also become hindered.

A person can learn how to *act* normal in order to belong, masking their insecurities. They may want connection but still protect their wounded and frozen essence on the inside. Emotional walls keep people from getting close to their true self. They may allow surface relationships with people or things to validate some sense of worth yet remain in a silent mode of self-protection. Mental disorders may begin as they continually detach from their true core. Emotional wounds may not easily be exposed even to parents, yet fear has a foundational function in their future thought patterns and relationships. A sense of alienation remains deep within, as their thirsting soul longs for a love that satisfies their true yearning essence.

Coping strategies become alternative modalities for a sense of intimacy, power and control. Instead of coping and remaining damaged, they need to identify those deep-rooted fears, redefine them and literally grow new neurons in the brain. The only way is to relearn the privilege of being who they really are, believe that they are valuable and have the experience of being loved unconditionally.

> *"Fathers do not provoke your children to anger, but, bring them*
> *up in the discipline and instruction*
> *of the Lord."*
> *Ephesians 6:4 NASB*

Our Love Models

The way Mom and Dad treat each other will be a model of how a child treats others. Successful family relationships live by principles of love, trust and respect. This environment helps children feel secure, allowing them to blossom and become all they can be. The family structure and values also affect spiritual development. Like family, their essence can grow up through repentance, forgiveness, accountability and grace within the security of God's Fatherly love. A trusted authority deters children from making costly mistakes in life. Whether young or old, these principles still apply. Maturity is not defined as one's physical age. Emotional maturity is reflected through our authentic interactions with people. On a deeper level, spiritual maturity is defined by the measure our soul, affected by our essence, cooperates with God, our Father, in the call to love people. It not only means to know right, but also do right.

God's Role as Parent

Parents' roles influence a child's perception of God's authority whether they realize it or not. It's amazing how a young child sets their parent up as God as if they can do no wrong. Good parenting has the perfect balance of loving nurture and proper instruction through the roles of mother and father. Many family systems lack this balance today allowing fear to override a child's learning. Most of our emotional issues in life can benefit from God's Agape love framework, bringing that wise balance back in order.

Many think of God as a vengeful, fear-inducing ruler, eager to judge you for not living to a higher standard. Sadly, some do parent that way, which promotes a darker spiritual law, perpetuating shame, emotional isolation and separation from authority. We all need rules which provide safety and reliability. Aggressive or forceful authority is difficult to trust because it is easy to question the motive. It is a shame some have called this *Christian* leadership in the home. God, the Heavenly Father, offers pure and trustworthy love, worthy of obedience.

On the other hand, many think God only loves and does not enforce His governing laws or necessary judgment. God is also not a giver of everything a child wants just because they demand or think they are entitled to it either. He doesn't conform to our reality. Consequences for poor choices are to teach us to respect His laws. A lack of respect and structure in the home causes children to have a more self-centered ego, designing their own plan for selfish gain. God intended the perfect balance of His love and His laws to bless and support His creation. The original family was meant to represent such a place for children. Obedience within the foundation of His love, not fear, brings true liberty.

"Now the Lord is the Spirit, and where the Spirit of the Lord is, there is freedom."
2 Corinthians 3:17 ESV

When correction is implemented with love and consistency, the developing child can still emerge with unique talents, confidence and influence. Correction encourages self-control which welcomes better success in all areas of life. If parents were not skilled in developing these character- building virtues, God, the all-knowing parent, will allow life to influence our growth. His natural and spiritual laws support the development of self-control, empathy, accountability, confidence and upright character. Respectful operation of these commandments of love and directives prepares the child with an advantage in their spiritual calling as well. This helps maintain good relationships without separation and alienation from their physical and spiritual roots.

Children cannot know what they have never experienced. They perceive truth to be what their parents model. If they didn't perceive love, they are less likely to feel love. If they didn't perceive honorable authority, they won't understand how and why it works. If parents weren't skilled to develop character-building virtues, God, who is all-knowing, will target the underdeveloped character in order to develop their emotional and spiritual maturity. This perfectly balanced authority is needed in life in order to manifest His power in our lives. If we don't allow that, we restrict His authority and hinder the growth of our essence. It's better to learn such principles earlier than later. That's why our own maps are not always the territory.

Trusting Connections

People need a connection they can trust in order to grow. Giving of one's own self for the sake of the other shows how valuable a person is to them. Good parents are trustworthy and so is God's agape love. He personifies selfless love. When you know you are valued to such a degree, it's easier to recognize discrepancies in others. You will manage people wisely and use boundaries. All children deserve to grow up with such love, equipping them to discern the counterfeits of love.

I believe that innocent children have a right to the spiritual truth. What harm would there be telling them that there is a

Heavenly Father whose love for them never changes and is better than any love on earth, including their parents'? Why not offer them hope that God who lives in us gives us strength to get through the difficulties in life? They could learn that our friend Jesus is there to guide us from inside. They have great imaginations and what a great way to build their faith muscles! Children often grasp these simple truths better than we give them credit for because it bears witness to their pure, less-corrupted minds. They will eventually learn parents are not omnipresent or sovereign but they can connect anytime to the One who is. This offers a safe and loving friend to turn to when their emotions of fear try to overtake them.

> *"There is no fear in love. But perfect love drives out fear, because fear has to do with punishment. The one who fears is not made perfect in love."*
> *1 John 4:18 NIV*

Examine your early interpretations of family dynamics. Do you perceive God's authority in a similar fashion? Did you obey out of fear more than out of love? Here are some situations worth examining how the child within may have been affected:

- Strife and/or manipulation between parents
- Burdening the children with parents' issues
- Neglecting the child's feelings, lacking communication to resolve them
- Lack of validation or mercy from either parent
- A perfectionist parent who was overly critical
- Either a lack of accountability or an excessive amount of responsibility
- A lack of open communication about emotions in the home
- Lack of connection with one or both parents
- An emotionally unavailable parent
- Lack of a positive role model from an absent parent
- Family secrets or lack of wise counsel about changes affecting children
- Child abuse in any form: sexual, emotional,

       verbal, physical, mental or neglect
- Alcoholism or other addictive patterns in the home
- Frequent angry outbursts from a parent

Did you have to earn your love? Did you have to hide your home life from others? What patterns of thought mapped out how you survived? Are you searching for a deeper connection with a person whose emotional style resembles your disengaged parent?

If you covered up your problems at home, this can lead to a dual personality, disconnected from the truth of your condition and your true essence. If you carried the unfair burdens of wounded parents and a broken home, you may still be operating in a role which seems to bring a sense of security in your present relationship.

Your birth order, the culture and even the tendencies passed down from your ancestors all contribute to how you gained a sense of value. Some of what you learn builds strengths and talents yet there may be tendencies laced with iniquity. If there was fear motivating you, God intends to re-build that faulty foundation into one of true love, faith and trust. He will help sort out the wheat from the tares to find the real you. It's imperative to believe that God loves you, is pursuing you and wants your true essence and identity to bloom as you understand how darkness has affected you.

> *"Though my father and mother forsake me,*
> *the Lord will receive me."*
> *Psalm 27:10 NIV*

Chapter 2

Adolescent Coping

I VISITED MY mom and sister every month or so on weekends. She and Yvette relocated to Windsor and moved eight times throughout the downtown areas over the next few years. She rented places that she could afford, which led us kids to roam some areas which were not safe. One morning we woke to find a drunken man asleep on our porch. It was a very different life compared to the farm, with different kinds of danger and city noise. Yvette had been beat up by a group of cruel and intimidating girls on her way home from school. Every time I returned home to my dad's I felt so bad that I couldn't watch over my sister more and protect her from bullies.

At fourteen years old, feeling pressured by one of my cousin Karlene's friends, I began to smoke cigarettes. It eventually became a habit and provided a means of relieving tension. It was the normal lifestyle anyways, smoking with friends, like my mom and most of her relatives on her side.

Every Sunday, the aunts, uncles and cousins came to my Pepe's house. He was a mean man with a deep voice and always had a beer in front of him. My cousins and I feared him. All of my aunts and uncles were heavy drinkers; most of them smoked marijuana, played poker and other games gambling with money. At times things would get out of hand and some aunts and uncles got loud and violent with each other. I remember a few times

Yvette and I were locked in a bedroom as we heard screaming, scuffling and glass breaking. We'd get let out when it was safe and saw the aftermath of injuries and Aunt Betty breathing in a paper bag from a panic attack.

I hung out with the crowd at school who liked to smoke, drink alcohol, and party too. It seemed fun at that time to get lost in a state that separated me from reality in some way, as if it lessened the pain of something hurting deep inside me. It was a strange yet uninhibited connection with those experiencing the same altered state. It was easier to not think of the consequence of my actions, because the thrill was worth it, whatever that entailed. I had developed an "I don't care" attitude. At times I felt impulsively drawn for attention from men. I curiously felt I had a sense of value when I did.

Back at home on the farm, some of my early work experiences were in the fields planting and picking vegetables, working in greenhouses, a canning factory, and corn detasselling. I did a lot of mechanical and body work and building and repair work as my dad was skilled in these areas. I think that I was the boy he never had. I began to resent all the hard work around the property. My efforts seemed in vain and without appreciation.

I had become less concerned and attentive toward my dad for many reasons. He sold the car I was working on after leading me to believe that it was my future car, which was my allowance. I realized by that time that my dad had women issues and his multiple relationships led me to joke about him to my friends and my mom's family. I felt he deserved to be laughed about. Besides, I began to believe that what he did to me when I was younger wasn't right. I didn't tell him about my feelings or what kind of partying went on with my mom's family, or with my friends. We never talked about relationships, or how I was managing with people in my life. Besides, he was also busy with his newest live-in girlfriend, Heather, who was a secretary at my high school. She stayed at our house the longest, with her son Clayton. Life seemed closest to normal when they lived with us. She would cook great meals and helped with the house and we did get along quite well. The only time I was upset with her was when she told my dad that she had to pick me up from the police station one day.

On one of my weekend adventures at my mom's, I met a co-worker of hers named "Tim," who came over to visit us and bring over some *good stuff* to smoke. He soon became my new boyfriend and we saw each other every weekend. Either he would drive an hour to the countryside where I lived, or I would spend weekends at my mom's or at his apartment which was at that time in Windsor.

One night, after we used several substances, evidenced throughout Tim's car, he sped to get me home since it was past my curfew. Noticing police lights behind him, Tim tried to lose the police as they gave chase. We ended up in a ditch after he lost control around a bend in the highway. Before we could exit the car there were guns pointed at us and 3 police cars around us. We were taken to the police station where I later was picked up by my dad and his then girlfriend, Bonnie.

I began to drive Tim's car to school since he got his license suspended. One day, as I was filling the radiator with a jug of water before heading to school, my dad approached me. He told me, "As long as you're living at this house, you're not allowed to see that guy!"

I responded, "Well, I'm moving out then!"

I shifted the car in drive using only the attached vice grips on the steering column, and I drove away, feeling proud of my response. I felt I was finally taking charge of my life. I didn't care that he might have felt angry or hurt. It was one of the most liberating feelings in my life at that point.

I decided to move away from home and transferred halfway through twelfth grade to a Windsor high school to be sure to get my diploma. This way I would also continue to see Tim. I moved in with him and I began attending beauty school so that I could be working soon, and begin making an income on my own.

During this time there was plenty of exposure to all kinds of mind-altering substances. Tim's brother, a heavy user and substance dealer, frequented our place with all we would need, even if we wanted to make some money selling, which I did here and there. Socializing with our friends and my mom's family, playing cards or video games usually included getting high.

After almost two years, I knew that I couldn't keep going on like this. The lifestyle became routine, and I began to feel stuck there, and my life with Tim was going nowhere. Tim was not hearing my concern and I also suspected he was not being honest and exclusive to me. The only way to move on from this was to move out on my own and take charge of my life again, so I found an apartment to live on my own and made a new start.

Adolescent Coping
Key Points

"'Fitting in' is about assessing a situation and becoming who you need to be to be accepted. Belonging, on the other hand, doesn't require us to change who we are; it requires us to be who we are."

Brene Brown, The Gifts of Imperfection

Learning Toxic Patterns

Because of this imperfect world, our own methods of coping can mold us into who we think we are or who others want us to be. Our identity evolves into our culture for acceptance and strength, while we still yearn to be loved, valued and belong for who we are inside. Those coping mechanisms and supporting strategies inhibit us from becoming free within our true essence. Over time, these patterns may become embedded in our thought processes contributing to mythical thinking. Our ego serves to house the façade, mediating the conscious with the unconscious. We develop a counterfeit version of our genuine essence, some of us becoming quite chameleonic for acceptance.

Coping behaviors can become difficult to undo, especially when they've had a genetic influence or validation from them. Deeper yet are pre-adolescent wounds from violation in childhood. Without being guided through the healing with proper love and security, the wounded soul is the target for more pain.

Sexual violation prompts a deeper God-created response in the victim. This may cause a yearning for sexual intimacy sooner than emotional maturity is attained. Soul ties create emotional and spiritual bonds with a person, affecting our total being with profound effect. This may generate more intense needs for a relationship or a fear of intimacy. Substances and addictive habits may even take the place of an emotionally intimate relationship.

An early foundation that lacked self-discipline, love and direction is an open door for exploring habits that offer a sense of temporary gratification. Substances can seem to become a refuge from life's emotional pressures. Distorted sexual intimacy, recently labelled as "sextimacy, offers a very temporary sense of connection, satisfying the excess of adrenaline. Sexual relationships are often developed before an equal balance of emotional and spiritual are attained because the chemicals responsible for mature judgement have been pushed off by adrenaline. Within such, feelings of emptiness and insignificance will often cycle to more devaluing intimate encounters for short-lived significance.

Some young adults have the false belief that their value comes from their actions or their appearance so they are drawn to people who are also emotionally and spiritually underdeveloped. Sadly, many are glad takers, usually unaware of the pain they contribute to and perpetuate. Unhealthy connections and temporary fixes cause individuals to remain stuck, leaving a void inside the soul for a love that leads to true security and an unhindered identity.

Mapping Life from Insecurity

Tough love can be challenging for both parent and teen. If both parents can balance the house rules with respectful loving guidance, their home offers a sense of security, predictability and respect. Teens should not be nursed like babies nor taken for granted. Teenagers without value-based rules in their home tend to enter relationships according to their impulsive desires. They will mold their own truth based on their underdeveloped ego. A lack of a higher reality of the truth disempowers people from maturing their essence and developing good character. This is how the entitlement mentality originated.

People are still accountable for their choices to a higher authority as adults. The longer an unrestrained person lives, the more self-focused they become. Eventually their conscience becomes seared because denial becomes weaved into their norm. Without a teachable attitude and a willingness to cooperate, rebellion continues, looking for more self-indulging vanities. Instant gratification, false core beliefs and an unrestrained ego will someday lead to frustration, cynicism, hopelessness, loneliness or even suicide. I believe many adults are stuck in this stage of maturity because they left home emotionally underdeveloped. They were not adequately taught to recognize and resolve conflicts from wounds in childhood. The natural bent is to conceal their stuck essence with a *pseudo-personality*.

The inherent need to connect and belong will cause a person to adapt to their peers while keeping their true identity frozen. The wounds of childhood allow an alternate foundation to form an acceptable identity built on fear instead of on love. In order for that to be sustained, it continues to wall in or isolate the true self, never exposing the inner child. They may forge a relationship with another familiar underdeveloped soul in order to attempt to finish an incomplete work within themselves.

"And I will be your Father, and you will be my sons and daughters, says the Lord Almighty."
2 Corinthians 6:18 NIV

What happened to the brain?

Puberty is the age of developing ethical accountability. At this stage, children grasp their cultural norms while they are still teachable. In adolescence, the brain begins to release three chemicals during puberty: serotonin, dopamine and norepinephrine. These chemicals help with rational, logical and emotional decisions, while their hormones are also changing. This explains why their behaviour changes as they begin to make sense of their experiences.

Trauma such as sexual and physical abuse or deep rejection that occurred before puberty can actually change the brain's chemistry during this phase. Those adolescents may feel disturbing confusion as they try to make sense of their discomfort when certain emotions arise or when they become vulnerable. The heightened emotions re-ignite a fight-or-flight response. This sudden release of adrenaline serves to protect the person from something such as an authority figure or emotional intimacy. Anytime they feel vulnerable, controlled or threatened, the emotional memory re-ignites the flow of adrenaline; therefore the dopamine, serotonin and norepinephrine cannot release as they would normally. They are simply trying to protect themselves instead of connecting and trusting which causes them to remain underdeveloped. This repetitive response reinforces dysfunctional neural pathways, which becomes their normal way of functioning. They have not experienced a healthy balance of love, trust and wisdom, so subsequently their beliefs and behavior cannot change unless they are open and teachable. They may even avoid gaining insight about their condition because they doubt any authority apart from their own. The body continues to grow yet the mind remains only as mature as the traumatic experience left it.

Imbalances in the brain may contribute to emotional and relational problems, but are sometimes not recognized until years later. Emptiness and loneliness may easily lead them to co-dependent and abusive relationships. Many forfeit their own personal growth or they simply don't have the tools or are not seeking out healthier relationships. They don't know what complete feels like and have not been able to recover their lost essence.

"For this reason God sends them a powerful delusion so that they will believe the lie."
1 Thessalonians 2:11 NIV

"For those who live according to the flesh set their minds on the things of the flesh, but those who live according to the Spirit set their minds on the things of the Spirit. For to set the mind on the flesh is death, but to set the mind on the Spirit is life and peace."
Romans 8:5-6 ESV

Chapter 3

Intimacy with God

"Draw near unto God and He will draw near to you."
James 4:8 NKJV

My first hairstylist job was at the Golden Razor in Windsor, which met the expenses of an apartment my own. I was back in charge of my own life since breaking up with Tim. I had a new beginning, a new attitude, a nice car and new friends at work. I fashioned myself with more class and professionalism compared to the once cowgirl-like ruggedness. I considered pursuing a psychology degree, after I saved up enough money to pay for school. I was building a large clientele, feeling valued when I could give them a great look. The weekends were filled with socializing, dancing and partying with my friends and sometimes with my mom and Aunt Margaret. I vacationed to the Bahamas with a girlfriend I worked with.

No matter how much fun I tried to have, I always felt incomplete and alone deep inside. I was always searching for a meaningful connection with a man but ended up finding only superficial intimacy. In a new relationship, I would seem to live on an emotional high for a while but it was always temporary, leaving only feelings of being used, disappointed or turned off by some unimportant imperfection in a guy. My heart was broken many times and I broke some hearts of others too.

I knew that my life was different than others because of my past. Many women were free to be who they really were, and I didn't have that transparency. I always felt that I was hiding the real me and replicated others' styles. Depression haunted me during the times I was not *high* on a relationship or on something else to numb the pain. Periods of hopelessness hovered over me like a dark cloud. I feared people would see through the confident façade that I was insecure, lonely and empty.

I mastered the art of looking great on the outside which was easy to do as a beauty industry professional. As an artist and people pleaser, I felt a sense of validation as I helped make people feel better about themselves. Deep inside I longed to feel complete and wanted to live with confidence. If I had answers through the fog of confusion, I could experience the freedom to just be me.

My search led me to self-help books, giving me some insight about my life through topics of positive thinking, enlightenment through New Age spirituality and psychology. I wanted to learn all I could to deal with the pain of my past and to figure out what was wrong with me. There was a measure of confidence gained from being successful and positive, but most of all I concluded that life without healthy relationships still leaves a person empty. I wanted to feel connected and really belong. This only fueled a longing for my own family one day; I would rewrite my past and plan a better future of my own. *How do I get there?* It was more like a dream, an unattainable fairytale. The more I thought of it, the more I feared loneliness. I longed for that peace and simplicity, before my family was shattered by divorce.

I wanted to calm the anger and disappointment I had toward my dad and other people around me who didn't deserve my wrath when I had a bad day. I didn't like who I was and I became frustrated doing the same wrong things to myself and others. I began to hate the fact that I lacked control over the two packs of cigarettes a day I was smoking, and that I was using marijuana here and there. It was not only bad for my health, but I thought it made me appear to be a weak and unrestrained person which I knew that, deep down, I was not. Turning to smoking was only keeping me from turning to something else, and if I didn't quit, I may never know what that something else was. I wanted truth and I couldn't find it anywhere in my life.

I decided that my New Year's resolution was to quit all smoking, cold turkey. I would never go back, no matter what. I was twenty-one years old and it was time to take charge of my life again. I chose to avoid the bar scene where smoking always accompanied drinking and reckless decisions. There were many invitations and temptations to continue living the way I'd been but I resisted. I was succeeding, although I hated feeling alone and having to be doing something all the time, never sitting still. I painted and fixed up my apartment, exercised excessively, and worked as many hours as possible just to keep busy.

At times I would find myself crying for no reason or crying easily over something on television. I felt lonely yet I didn't want anyone around to interrupt whatever I was searching for. Nobody would understand anyhow. I knew that answers were coming, because at times I had such a clear perspective, as if God was illuminating truth behind everything. I sensed a presence about my life as if God was reaching for me to take His hand to show me the way home, but not the one I lost. I began to discern people differently. Everything had an origin, from light or dark, good or evil, love or hate.

I shared my thoughts with Donna, a co-worker and friend, and I knew that she had family members who were Christian ministers. Her mom gave Donna a book that she suggested that I read, titled *200 of Life's Most Probing Questions* written by Pat Robertson. I began to read it and found answers through scriptures in the Bible that lined up with the questions I had in life at that time. They brought more enlightenment and clarity, confirming the reality of my experiences and thoughts. The scripture references were so simple but so profound to me, coming alive as they spoke to my longing heart. Any question I had about God, the meaning of my hardships, my future and eternity were answered with significant truth, hope and love. Beyond the words I was reading was a sense of entering the unknown. It felt like I'd found Gods divine peace, love and presence which transcended mental and physical knowledge. I felt high with awareness, yet not influenced by a substance.

I wondered, *Why hasn't anyone ever told me about this? Who else in this world knows what I'm sensing? If other people know about this, then why haven't I ever heard about it? I'd seen the dark side most of my life, so perhaps that's why I'm able to see the light.* Nothing had ever made more sense to me or felt so right and good. I wanted to tell someone but I knew it would be hard to explain if they had never experienced it themselves.

I knew that Satan is real and he's focused on keeping people from believing in the love I'd found. I could see how people were not even aware of his evil schemes. It was all normal to them. He was affecting their relationships, habits and goals. It was clear that his influence had been a huge part of my life as I remembered the dark sinister depression and despair. It was all gone. I have a purpose now. I want to love people and give them hope. The other things I longed for felt empty, but this was satisfying like nothing else. This new way of thinking and feeling was so altered, yet more real than ever; I wanted to stay high on it forever.

> *"And you shall seek me and find me when you search for me*
> *with all your heart."*
> *Jeremiah 29:13 NKJV*

I had heard about Jesus's death on the cross but until this, I'd never realized what it meant to me and my life. I did not know what salvation was or that it was that easy—to just open the door of my heart to Him. I never knew that accepting His sacrificial act of love and dying for me could give me such an experience. It felt as if this new life started living inside and through me, satisfying the longing within me that I always had, yet never could define or explain. It gave me a confidence of my eternal security that I never knew was attainable. I didn't fear death like I had earlier. The power that raised Jesus from the grave actually came alive inside of me, simply because I asked for it! It was like a spiritual incarnation of His life into my soul.

I cried so often but not because I was sad, but because the release of pains from the past that I held inside seemed to be met with healing love from God. I had never felt so free inside. I wasn't concerned any longer about things that really didn't matter. I didn't want anything to get in the way of this connection that I knew was with God Himself.

The love inside began to free me from darkness, fear and

shame. I was compelled to love instead of hate. I looked for opportunities to show others how valuable they were. I knew I tapped into a spiritual reality, so much greater than I had ever known.

This was not just an emotional experience. It also became tangible in ways that only God could orchestrate. He used people, music and scriptures to validate the change of heart I was experiencing.

I had a new solid and secure foundation. It would forever mark my heart and life. My longing heart found its home. I hoped this connection to God would never change, yet I sensed it wouldn't be like this forever. There was a darkness looming around; I could sense it. It was like it wanted my newfound truth buried again, hidden behind familiar blinders I knew too well.

"For you have died and your life is hidden in Christ."
Colossians 3:3 NASB

Intimacy with God
Key Points

"Our brains are wired for love and we learn fear.
Fear is not normal."
Dr. Caroline Leaf

Adopted to Function in Love

There are dominant circuits in the brain which function for love. If we are made in Gods image, we were made to function and grow by love without shame or pride affecting our true selves. That was the plan from the beginning before deception interrupted the intimate union with God and each other. When the natural function for love becomes tainted, the need for pure love still leaves us feeling incomplete as we cover our true condition. In order to recover our true essence and divine destiny, we need a greater love than the type known on earth, a love that will sanctify, purify and heal the parts that are broken. It operates through God's Spirit to our spirit but our soul became more accustomed to listening to our emotions, taking us away from our original essence. This requires an overhaul of anything we believed that was untrue about us and God. It will take trials and tests to purify your essence. Sadly, Satan uses his best tool, deception, to keep people from this very foundational truth about their true condition. He wants you alienated from your Heavenly Father and your true self. On a positive note, Christ came to restore that union and, through His obedience to the Father, He succeeded in His mission and only those who enter through the veil (His sacrifice) will experience this oneness with Him. See Hebrews 10:19-20.

> *"The glory that you have given me I have given to them that they may be one even as we are one. I in them and you in me that they may become perfectly one so that the world may know that you sent me and loved them even as you have loved me."*
> *John 17:22-23 ESV*

This concept is a mystery to unbelievers. They mentally cannot grasp this spiritual concept which is why they think believers are the ones off base (see Ephesians 3:4). Just because they don't believe, does not make what is hidden from them untrue.

In order to recover our pure innocent essence, it takes great abandon, faith, willingness and intimacy on our part. Intimacy in this context means *into – me – see*. That point of *emotional nakedness* is different for everyone because of family dynamics and individual processing. Some discover their essence early in life and some after great tragedy or near death. Sadly, many never recover it at all, rejecting the very One who longs to bring their essence back to life.

Separated by Shame, Fear and Deception

Mankind's intimacy with God was lost in the Garden of Eden when His authority was discounted. Whether or not a person believes there was such a garden, mankind's need to restore that intimacy with God has become paramount as these truths are fading in the fog of what's right anymore. Many people today are as orphans—alienated from God, their original spiritual Father, lacking the proper love and guidance needed to develop their essence. Without His loving security, fear and pride have greater influence on the soul. Isolating the wounded essence only alienates us from the very One who longs to restore it.

Prisons are filled with people who acted out because of a lack of balanced intimate authority in childhood. Others remain in their own emotional prison, orphaned spiritually, unknowingly yearning for an original intimacy restored.

Since the day we were born, we had a need to belong, feel valuable and to be connected through relationships. Relationships also cause wounds, affecting how we bond. Therefore, it will take the right relationship to restore our value. Relationships may lack the safe emotional intimacy we seek in others. Until the connection with God is realized, we involuntarily thirst for this restoration in harmful ways. This causes further alienation and toxicity to our soul.

Shame, pride and fear are rooted in flesh and blood. They caused separation from God in the beginning. God wants that original intimacy back with His people. Through our trials, we must learn to trust, then we can be reconciled back to God through spiritual adoption. Jesus Himself said:

> *"That which is born of the flesh is flesh and that which is born of the spirit is spirit."*
> *John 3:6 ESV*

The areas of our wounded soul will be a target for healing and a deeper truth to be revealed. Wounds often get covered with lies if they were not nurtured back to through love. Knowing the God of true love provides a safe place for our true essence and souls to progress on the road to peace, truth and amazing love. He created our heart and He bids it to belong to Him first. He knows its design better than anyone, including you. He has given us all the tools to become whole and complete. Christ willingly died to bring back that intimate connection with God. He removed the barrier of our sins which separated us from Him so that we may come to Him without shame. This is the key to being free within all future relationships and the beginning of finding your true self. Our hidden pain still does affect our relationships. Nothing can stop His love for us, but we close the door to it because the territory is unfamiliar. We need to believe, be teachable and open our souls and hearts to His love just as a child dependent on their father and mother. In doing so, you will overcome every obstacle personally and relationally.

"I have said these things to you, that in me you may have peace. In the world you will have tribulation. But take heart, I have overcome the world."
John 16:33 ESV

We are made up of three parts; we are a spirit, we have a soul and we live in a body. We have a destiny to fulfill and it takes all three parts of our being to live it out here on earth. What this physical world has to offer will not completely satisfy us because we are spiritual beings. We rely so much on our physical senses and the world around us that it's easy to pay less attention to growing our spiritual self which affects our emotional and physical essence.

Many believe that Jesus came to earth and died on a cross, yet not everyone understands what was accomplished for mankind. The purpose for Christ coming to earth and dying was to restore the intimate union with our Heavenly Father. There is no other way to attain it. Divine connection with God was lost in the Garden of Eden because of the power to choose our own way. Jesus also was given the power to choose, but He also knew obedience out of love and not out of fear which tainted mankind. He also became acquainted with all human suffering yet chose to remain obedient, unlike the rebellion against God in the original Garden. By Jesus's obedience, we have been given access to the same grace to overcome sin, to follow our Abba Father and fulfil His abundant call on our lives. Over time and experience, we are united again to a freedom within our purifying essence and uninhibited oneness with God.

The greatest miracle known to humanity was that Jesus conquered death's power at the cross and God raised Him from the grave. Talk about high vibrations, laws of attraction and quantum physics! Not only was there victory over death, but He was the atonement for our sins and its power over us. In other words, our sins have not stopped God from loving us. Who on earth can love unconditionally like that? Christ took the blame, allowing us to be blameless, as if we'd never sinned. His act of selfless love brought us back to a state of purity and connection to the Father, just as when sin affected our essence in childhood. You don't earn it or sacrifice for it, just receive His sacrificial gift of pure love. No wonder the salvation experience is beyond comprehension, proving that even our relationships are also multidimensional.

Why not let God help you recover your lost essence, just as the deserving child you were before sin tainted it? Simply open the door of your heart to Him who is trustworthy and be willing to work together to break the curse of the *orphaned spirit* and be *adopted and fostered* to grow up in your true essence.

> *"For as many as are led by the Spirit of God, they are the sons of God. For ye have not received the spirit of bondage again to fear; but ye have received the Spirit of adoption, whereby we cry, Abba, Father. The Spirit itself beareth witness with our spirit, that we are the children of God: And if children, then heirs of God, and joint heirs with Christ; if so be that we suffer with him, that we may be also glorified together."*
> *Romans 8:14-17 KJV*

Like me, some people can feel a spiritual change more tangibly. If darkness had a hold and the law of sin dominated so much of our lives, an impartation of love and truth is very real. Not everyone experiences a vivid enlightenment in such a way. Opening the heart's door is only the beginning of a lifelong process. If a person had the advantage of having emotionally intelligent parents, their relationships may also benefit having a more positive framework. Some of us have to relive our past, requiring a total makeover of the soul. God's goal is for us to be fully restored into who He created us to be.

Upon salvation, a major conflict begins. Our insecurities relating to wounds and weakness from our past will often pull us away from growing our essence, making it a longer process or even a neglected one, depending on our ability to relinquish some control. This becomes a matter of trust and obedience, just as a child guided by parents all over again. God's authority and justice can only work according to the surrender of our will to His. This can be difficult without proper spiritual guidance, because stronger pathways in the brain have established, which subconsciously protect the child within who may still have trust issues or wants to do life their way. To put it bluntly, our carnality is very persuasive.

Faith and trust activates the gift of grace. Fear and control prevent the function of grace in us. The appropriate measure of grace is a gift from God given to us to renew our minds from the old to the new. Grace can only be activated by our willingness to follow His leading, aligning our surrendered soul to His truth. No matter how much confusion has entangled our lives, grace is there to help. It's a power worth tapping in to; yet to function constantly in it would mean you were equal to Christ, which cannot be so. Growing in grace takes a lifetime. I'm happy to see that many Christians today are grasping the foundational need to exchange our power for His. In reference to what was stolen from those suffering from arrested development, it's like grace replaces the voids where mature judgement was not developed. Understanding the power of grace allows the brain to develop the neural pathways for logical and wise thinking before reacting. This is also spiritual and emotional intelligence at work. This confirms that His ways are higher than our ways.

"Moreover the law entered, that the offence might abound. But where sin abounded, grace did much more abound."
Romans 5:20 KJV

Trials are Pre-cursors to Soul Freedom

There is a reason for your life's battles. They are sanctioned for your spiritual good, ensuring a purpose; and Jesus's life, death and resurrection proves this. Jesus spent His life showing and teaching us how God's government works, how to discern the errors of mankind and how to grow spiritually and intimately with people.

Learning to work with God is a very different system of government than the ones we know on earth. It's no wonder Christians are misunderstood.

Earthly government is tainted with competition, corruption and distrust. In academics we are graded or scored with an IQ. This mentality transfers into churches as people continue to be graded for good-ness or righteousness which is still far from how God sees us.

In God's government, we are not graded by our good works but by the working of His grace and power working through us. Our brains have functioned for years by these earthy judging principles. Spiritual principles are counter-intuitive. We are spiritual beings subjected to spiritual laws that also affect the results. Our lives no longer embody a *survival of the fittest* mentality or ego-boosting fixes that our culture baits us to function in. God's *higher law* of love is the greatest power available to us. His relational principles work on a different level than what we are familiar with on earth. Even modern mental science is advancing closer to this reality of our complete psyche being in need for emotional and even spiritual connection to something greater than ourselves. Our brains actually function better because of this. God knew what He was doing when He made the brain capable of recovering one's essence lost childhood. He prepared us to experience His divine truth in our carnal minds. Science now confirms the fact that we can reprogram our own brain according to our new truth. This is why the Bible frequently mentions being; "renewed in the spirit of our minds." Ephesians 4:23 ESV

It's much more complex than it sounds. Renewing the mind is a huge feat but the only *perfect* way to recover our lost essence. It will involve pain, but when it leads to surrender to the One who *is* pure love, there is nothing like it that can bring full recovery to our essence. Otherwise our essence without His grace remains built on our own faulty foundation, formed with childish, intellectual and carnal perceptions that still limit our growth. We must understand the role of the Holy Spirit in our lives. We cannot do this on our own.

> *"Now the Lord is the Spirit, and where the Spirit of the Lord is, there is liberty."*
>
> *2 Corinthians 3:17 NASB*

Renewing the Mind with Love and Truth

"I will give them an undivided heart and put a new spirit in them; I will remove from them their heart of stone and give them a heart of flesh."
Ezekiel 11:19 NIV

Our spiritual identity and true essence matures over time as we yield our familiar old nature to our new nature. This process is called *sanctification* in Christianity. Everything we knew from before takes on a different meaning which can be confusing for some. The way it works, results from receiving what's been done for us, not from what we do alone. People are more familiar with laws and cultural standards to achieve success and are naturally looking to fit in. The flesh and soul begin to war with the Spirit and essence because they are two different models. Since our minds think we have to control ourselves, many religious people get into following rules, thinking that's how they should act. That's a big inaccuracy and it's no wonder Christianity has its critics. Acceptable behavior is positive, but not the only means by which righteous purity is attained. Grace must be equally in the mix, allowing the Holy Spirit to lead us. If not, it remains tainted and people detect this. This is *legalism, Christianese* or *religion without relationship.*

Many people operate in their own uprightness and not in the gift of grace. Grace is defined in the context of this book as the power to obey God. We can't make ourselves holy or pure by going through the motions of religion, legalism and Christ-likeness. This is labelled as *works of righteousness* done through our own flesh. We are transformed to His likeness through faith and the grace to follow Him to do right, not our doing alone. Grace and works must go hand in hand; otherwise our expression is imbalanced, just as a child would receive imbalanced parenting, affecting their overall emotional health and relationships.

"He saved us, not because of works done by us in righteousness, but according to his own mercy, by the washing of regeneration and renewal of the Holy Spirit."
Titus 3:5 ESV

The renewal of our soul doesn't happen overnight and continues through our lifetime only as we allow and as we understand its function. Our soul must be in synergy with our spiritual essence to grow. It takes practice to allow faith, grace and obedience to affect our outcomes. Grace is a function of the Holy Spirit in us, enabling us to live out His purposes.

Through life's trials, the power of grace operates in us as we surrender our old and familiar self to recover our real self. This is just the beginning of soul freedom and experiencing life from our essence. Our true self now has a secure and trustworthy path, no longer governed by the effects of this world tearing us down, binding us up and wearing us out. Sounds wonderful, but it will not be easy. It takes emotional pain and frequent surrender of our will to re-learn old thinking patterns. Some of us put up a fight when control was our means to survive, not knowing our own emotions still enslave us from childhood. A person with a frozen essence can't easily leave their heart wide open to a God they have never known with their physical senses. Our faith will be tried through fires of affliction in order to be refined. It also means trusting God when life doesn't make sense. Faith isn't pure faith until it's all you are holding on to. That is the only secure foundation and the one which prepares us for heaven. By accepting this invitation on earth, we allow our true essence to be guided through this life, also allowing His kingdom to come on earth through you (see Matthew 6:10). The goal of His Spirit is to show you anything false about your identity.

> *"Knowing this, that our old self was crucified with Him, that our body of sin might be done away with, that we should no longer be slaves to sin."*
> *Romans 6:6 NASB*

There are many factors that will affect our spiritual growth and maturity of our essence. You may have a lifetime of coping mechanisms that seemed to work just fine for a while, but may still need some re-working to recover a lost or frozen essence. Through all the processes, God's love for you will never change. He will target the areas which keep you from His love, wisdom and truth because He loves us. Every area of weakness will eventually be an area of strength and some areas where you think you are strong may also need to be surrendered. I pray that as you continue to read, you are teachable. Your Heavenly Father really does know best.

In the next seven chapters, I will reveal some common obstacles to attaining true freedom and how they play out in our relationships. God lets us explore and test His truths for ourselves. They should cause us to question, study and practice so that we may grow wise. Wounded doesn't mean broken. True brokenness in our soul is required for true surrender. True surrender requires faith, trust and relationship. As a fostered child of God, these trials should lead us to live within our essence, preparing us for our destiny. The insights will offer practical application for the mind as well as deeper wisdom for your spirit.

"I have been crucified with Christ. It is no longer I who live but Christ who lives in me. And the life I know live in the flesh I live by faith in the Son of God who loved me and gave himself for me."
Galatians 2:20 ESV

Chapter 4

Unforgiveness: A Costly Trap

I SHARED MY experience with my mother and sister. I was surprised when my mom told me that she had a closer relationship with God years ago and she said maybe this was time to rediscover what that was again. My sister was also experiencing a spiritual awakening through a friend who shared this knowledge. It was as if God was doing the same work in all of us at the same time.

Easter morning came and my mom turned on the television and joked that it's time for church as we watched an Easter Sunday message in our pajamas. The minister spoke a message of Christ's love and of His death and resurrection which seemed so relevant to my recent experience. As we listened and watched, an intense beam of light radiated in the room as if it was confirming to us the reality of God's love and presence. It was as if He was telling us, *What you are hearing and experiencing is truly from me.* Each of us felt a presence of love so powerfully that we became overwhelmed with tears. It was a very tangible experience.

We decided that we needed to learn more about what we were experiencing. Perhaps there was a place to get some good bible teaching. We considered going to church, but where should we start with so many to choose from?

One day my sister, my mom and I went out for dinner after

we had bought a small house so we could all live together. As we sat, we decided that we should pray and ask God where to go to church. As we were eating and talking, a lady named Rosie Adlington sat at the table next to us with her husband and a young man, leaned over and struck up a conversation with us. Well, that conversation led us to an invitation to visit their church, Windsor Christian Fellowship.

It was interesting that we did just pray for His direction on this matter! We began to attend there regularly, meeting people that genuinely cared about seeing us grow in this new life that we were experiencing. It was clear to us that it was best to avoid the old way of life, the drinking, smoking and even the people associated with it in order to stay focused on a better path. I'm sure that many of the family members thought that we had gone off the deep end with our involvement with church. It was difficult holding back from talking about our spiritual awakening, especially to those we cared about.

We attended many church functions and got involved in the Singles Group to get acquainted with people and make some stable friends. It was a time of learning and healing. We each went to see a counselor because of the darkness and struggles from our past. My mom's childhood was horrible. Her alcoholic father had come back from the war in 1945 to eventually ten kids, my mom being the first girl and second-oldest child. She had to quit school in ninth grade to help her mom with responsibilities of caring for her siblings. They all suffered beatings by their father. The girls were all sexually molested by him. My mom moved out as soon as she could and knew she would never marry an alcoholic like her dad. There was little help in those days, and now, experiencing the power of God, this was her time to find healing for herself and hopefully her family, from those horrible memories.

> *"Like newborn babies, crave spiritual milk, so that by it, you may grow up in your salvation."*
> *1 Peter 2:2 NIV*

I often found myself up at the church altar when Pastor Rick would give the invitation if anyone had a need for prayer. I wanted everything I could to grow spiritually strong. God gave me the grace to forgive my dad and I didn't want to hold him, or myself, captive to the cage of my bitterness any longer. Previously I had distanced myself from him, even when he was trying to be nice. He was finally making an effort to be somewhat involved in our lives. I really wanted everything God had in store for me and I wanted no roadblocks that would hinder His blessings to work in my life and that of my family's.

So, I shared with my dad all that was happening and told him that I forgave him for all he had done. I know this touched him deeply because it brought tears to his eyes. I wanted him to experience healing from his own past and experience a new spiritual life as well. In my heart I had forgiven him and it released him to know I truly had.

My sister Yvette met a young man at the church and they planned to marry. They invited Pastor Luke to take the opportunity where loved ones were gathered, to offer a path to salvation. Toward the end of their wedding ceremony, Pastor gave an invitation to receive Jesus as their personal savior. To our surprise, my dad raised his hand and was fighting back tears! It was one of the happiest days in my life. Pastor Luke encouraged him to come to church the following day, which he did. The church cheered when the Pastor announced what had happened the day before at Yvette's wedding and had my Dad stand up so everyone could see him. I almost could not believe this was happening! *Could this mean he and mom could finally get back together? Could it be that God was actually restoring my childhood dream?*

Dad started visiting our house a lot. It was strange to see my mom and dad affectionate toward each other after all the years had gone by, even though they were divorced at the time. This went on for only a month or so. My mom became uncomfortable about getting too involved again with my dad. Getting physically involved she feared might lead her off the path of her spiritual growth. My dad didn't understand this way of thinking and began to stay away more. The last church service he attended, he stood with me in the parking lot and said, "You guys are way ahead of me." We talked a few times after that about the differences we had on tithing, church attendance, the restrictions, the worship style and repetitive songs. It was obvious this was not what he wanted and maybe he thought we were quite extreme about being so involved. Perhaps we were, but we knew if we didn't hold on tight like it was our lifeline, our old life would be tugging us back.

Months went by and I felt so disappointed that God would allow things to get so close and then fall apart again. It was like an old wound resurfacing childhood memories. Jesus came to give us abundant life but I felt stuck in this new wound of disappointment. It slowly began to fester in crevices in my soul.

"So Jesus said to them, 'The light is among you for a little while longer. Walk while you have the light, lest darkness overtake you. The one who walks in the darkness does not know where he is going.'"
John 12:35 ESV

One Sunday my dad showed up at my church! It surprised me but also gave me a glimmer of hope that he'd changed his mind about what he had said. I soon came to learn that he was there to meet up with one of the single ladies in my church whom he'd met through a singles ad in the paper. I became so enraged that he was so insensitive to all of us, and he had no regard for what we might have been feeling. The more he dated women, the angrier I got at him. This was not the way the story was supposed to go, in my mind.

I continued going to church and staying connected but it seemed that I was losing that "first love" experience with God. I knew the high wouldn't last forever, just like a romance. It was important to me continue to go to church and still learn what I could. I pretended much of the time that nothing was wrong but I couldn't ignore the disappointment in my dad. I tried to accept what was and focus on my own life, get over my childhood fairytale of my parents reconciliation and look forward to my own family I would have some day. My dad and mom may never get back together and we may never be a normal family. I became impatient that I was not finding a good Christian man either. I was experiencing loneliness and felt unattractive. I saw my sister's life moving forward with a family of her own. Don't I deserve the same thing, God? I began to go through the motions on the outside, not coming to peace on the inside.

Unforgiveness: A Costly Trap
Key Points

We Need Emotions

We need emotions, both the good and the bad ones. We can allow them to make us bitter or better. Anger lets us know something is wrong inside of us. It is often a signal that is tied to feeling threatened or devalued. Anger is toxic to the soul and the body and one of the most testing emotional states to live in. When anger is associated with devaluing events in childhood, unforgiveness is easily weaved into the soul. The slightest event can re-ignite its flame inside.

Anger seems to be empowering to some people as if anger is their friend. It may invoke fear or defensiveness in others. Often, issues with authority are tied with anger. If the core essence was wounded by an authority figure in childhood, they may digress into harmful thought patterns and behaviors including depression, addictions and abuse. These unhealed wounds can erupt from childhood wounds for years later. As it festers, it causes division in relationships, even the one with God.

Roots of Anger

Inner healing is necessary to thoroughly re-define painful childhood memories at the core. Until then, it is difficult make sense of the overpowering emotions. Many of us have not learned relational skills nor have we developed mature reasoning about the issue causing anger. Even a new relationship with God can be stifled by these feelings because trust in God has not yet been experienced at that level. The familiar emotions of the delicate wounded child remain unprotected. The adrenaline rush guards our survival. The wounded memory causes the fight-or-flight response, kicking in adrenaline when we are threatened or frustrated emotionally. The core essence remains frozen in development because it can only grow safely when we can trust. The chemicals responsible for processing logic were held back by the adrenaline for survival, causing an imbalance in the brain. Rational judgement was not important; survival was. The essence remains frozen yet protected by emotional isolation, fear, anger or pride. We understand how abused animals are affected this way; well, so are humans.

When a person understands their value to their Heavenly Father and they realize their mind needs to be renewed, they can begin the healing process and begin to learn healthy intimacy. This may take many years to experience as many Christians begin their spiritual journey, still wounded inside, regardless of their enlightening salvation experience. We need to come to terms with hidden unresolved issues instead of being held captive by them. There is no other clear way to recovering our true essence.

Without experiencing inner healing and imparting some appropriate action, it's difficult to move forward and forgive. This is where so many people remain stuck. What we don't understand can make us confused. What we do understand can be fixed. There is much more to understand.

"My people are destroyed for lack of knowledge."
Hosea 4:6 KJV

Why is it hard to forgive?

- We are aware of the injustice and we feel trapped or helpless because of it
- We may feel a sense of control, which makes up for a moment when we had none
- We don't want to let our offender off the hook especially if there's been no punishment or sincere apology—it's just not fair
- Their harmful words or actions deserve punishment and/or correction
- We do not want to act like we are condoning their wrong behavior
- We haven't received recompense for the damage they caused
- We have yet to trust in God's justice, which is a process of growing in grace

There is a direct tie between forgiveness and wholeness. Forgiveness allows closure and spiritual strength to grow. It empowers you to move forward into emotional freedom. It is one of the most important stepping stones to any recovery and finding your true identity. On a spiritual note, unforgiveness binds you up and therefore limits heaven's influence in your life. Choosing to remain angry affects intimacy in relationships. It's harder to love when hate obstructs the flow.

Our true identity grows when we choose to trust God, just as Christ did. Trusting God frees us from emotional captivity. Grace will empower us as we surrender the unseen into God's just hands. Having faith and trust in God offers the power to endure every challenge.

"Whatsoever is bound on earth is bound in heaven. Whatsoever is loosed on earth is loosed in heaven."
Matthew 18:18 NIV

Positive Attributes of Forgiveness:

- We take responsibility for our own happiness instead of blaming others
- God's grace, which helped Christ forgive mankind; will divinely enable us to do the same
- We attract love instead of resisting it, allowing God to freely live in you
- You are no longer a victim but a victor and no longer held captive
- Releases God to bring justice in His way and timing through faith
- Frees you to experience a better, healthier and more meaningful life
- Shows evidence of true strength, wisdom and grace
- We no longer are the judge, therefore we can be forgiven by God who is the ultimate Judge

Chapter 5

Unresolved Issues

GOD, IF ONLY you could give me a glimpse into the future just to give me some hope! I thought. He had the perfect chance to give me a sign of hope at the wedding of one of my co-workers. I could catch the wedding bouquet and that would satisfy my question about my future and marriage, hopefully soon on the horizon. I remember the day and how I felt. I almost didn't attend this wedding. I was fighting depression, anger, weight gain and battling with a food addiction. I didn't like the idea that I was going alone to a wedding, again. The reason I did go was, *Maybe tonight I would have an answer. Maybe, I will catch the bouquet!*

As the time approached to catch the bouquet, all the single ladies gathered. I was up front and positioned in the middle. Kathy's bouquet was a bundle of bud roses which were soaked with water in the base they were arranged in. The bouquet didn't fly gracefully up in the air. It seemed as if it came like a baseball bat being thrown and came straight toward my face. Instinctively, I closed my eyes but held out my hands to catch it. I didn't know what hit me so hard on the nose, if it was someone's fist or the heavy bouquet filled with water, but it felt like my nose was broken. My face and hair were splashed with the water from the roses, and makeup and blood were on my fingers.

I looked to see the frenzy around me and the girl that ended up with the bouquet, so I walked discretely toward the restroom, feeling tears well up. I looked in the mirror and my nerves began to quiver as my nose began to swell. My hair was wet, my makeup was almost off and I began to sob. It was not just because it hurt, or the embarrassment, but most of all what it represented. The message was coming across very clear: *I get it. You, get married? Who would want you? You're such a loser! Just look at you! Give it up!* I thought to myself, *God, if you were caring enough about the ache in my heart, you could have not allowed this to happen! Well, I guess it could mean that it won't ever happen. Even God could care less. I would just have to learn to accept that too. Besides, not my will, but yours be done,* I thought. I felt that God had forsaken my dream. Not wanting to be mad at God, I became even angrier at my dad. My life seemed like it was getting worse, not better.

> *"He heals the brokenhearted and*
> *binds up their wounds."*
> *Psalm 147:3 ESV*

Unresolved Issues
Key Points

Emotional Events Trigger Past Wounds

Our minds are the control towers of our lives. Our thoughts are controlled by our emotional needs and our core beliefs. Emotions influence our behavior. Painful memories stored within the amygdala in the brain can re-activate former emotions when familiar events trigger them in adulthood. Inevitably, we can be driven again by fear, causing us to want full control our lives, guarding what we value. This is the case with arrested emotional development.

The hurt child within longs to be whole and secure but remains unfulfilled. We have not experienced the security from the love we seek. The deep need for love can cause us to reason our way into how and why life should go our own way. Governing self-will is not given over easily and can cause a wedge in any relationship including the one with God.

Controlling our own Mental Systems

The ego is the part of the psyche that has conscious control of behavior and is more in touch with external reality. If trust, love and security have not been established in the core of the person, the ego tends to override other judgments. Unfulfilled dreams from childhood can remain in the corners of the mind. The spiritually intimate connection with God weakens because the malnourished essence sanctions the flesh to love on its terms. The will has a need for control and fear becomes greater than the need to surrender it. Because it is difficult to grasp what is happening within the soul, confusion begins again. The only spiritually effective solution is total surrender of the will to God, allowing His grace to lift the fog of confusion. The ego may not be willing because trust and wisdom have not been established at such an emotionally intimate level.

A lack of trust in authority, including God's, leaves a person in an emotionally deprived state. A deeper intimacy must be developed in order to override these deep-rooted emotions. Because of this, people will find alternate means to cope. Slowly, deception allows for other self-sustaining means to be appealing. Think of the word "compromise." Remove "com" from "promise." God's promises are held back while we reject His guidance and turn to something we think will satisfy.

I had allowed fear and impatience to creep in because I wanted things to happen when they should according to what I idolized deep in my soul. I couldn't understand why things were turning out worse instead of better. I also didn't realize at the time that there was a hidden lesson in these mysterious events which one day would make sense.

Sadly, we may assume we're not worthy or that's just life, but fear and /or pride keep us from growing up emotionally and spiritually. Many lose spiritual strength and may begin to question their spiritual experiences as they succumb to the more intense cravings of the soul. The unresolved issues begin to surface and people will cope in familiar patterns from the past.

Some signals that unresolved issues may be hidden in your soul:

- Fear of being alone or lonely
- Self-blame, self-criticism or self-harm
- Depression
- Confusion
- Discouragement
- Extreme ups and downs
- Inability to tolerate conflict and intense feelings
- Feeling a lack of value, importance or purpose
- Needing to be in control of others
- Unable to communicate feelings
- Panic attacks, intense anxiety
- Jealousy

Stuck in Arrested Development

It's easy to get off course emotionally in an imperfect world. We all have been victims of Satan's schemes that blind us because of our emotions—the easiest way to get at our weaknesses. If the brain has already built the framework for previous maladaptive patterns, familiar emotions fit right in. This is how childhood trauma interferes with adult development. The brain communicates signals that cause a familiar rush of adrenaline that affects wise judgement, thus acting secondary to the immediate need. The damaged emotional root system distorts Gods original design to meet emotional needs. The person's altered reality becomes part of their maladaptive beliefs, causing people to get stuck in emotional and spiritual growth. We cannot change what we do not understand. God will never force His best if our souls cannot accept His love. Many today are wounded and don't even know it, keeping God's very best from them.

A qualified therapist or clergy with inner healing experience should be sought because it's hard to walk out painful childhood memories alone. Otherwise, the harder and more painful way to learn is to live through it again in order to clearly identify its source. Never be too stubborn against wise counsel. Be open about those deep wounds so they can heal properly. Be honest with God the Father and Jesus your friend about your feelings. He doesn't mind listening. Go ahead and tell Him you are jealous, impatient and fearful or whatever. Confess it and don't be ashamed of your feelings. As a loving parent and friend, He wants you to be real about the ache in your heart. Ask for and listen to His guidance. Pursue His will until you find peace. Ask Him for His grace to stay on course.

The pursuit of an unmet dream as innocent as a family living happily ever after can override our personal development. The dream literally becomes an idol. It's as if fear, which is so familiar, became a bigger part of the foundation, so one may idolize the thing that was lacking as a child. It makes sense in our own eyes. Trust begins to falter and then other methods of coping begin. In this story, both characters in the first marriage idolized that which was painfully lost in childhood.

Some maladaptive coping patterns are:

- Any form of addiction
- Isolation or disassociation
- Inappropriate attachments
- Self-harm
- Anger and/or aggression
- Perpetrating others
- Personality disorders
- Rescuing or enabling others
- Needing constant affirmation
- Constant criticism and blaming others

Let God speak to your heart about the pain of your past. He cares so deeply about them. Affirm yourself in scriptural promises because His words contain His power. Educate yourself to renew your mind with those truths. Your new reality will begin to unfold according to His plan in His time. Grace happens in you when faith and His word are at work. He wants an intimate relationship with you in order to prepare you for what lies ahead. Sin is a big deal and causes separation from God.

Don't give in to choices that lead to a wedge in your relationship with Him. He cares about your dream. Trust Him.

> *"For I know the thoughts that I think toward you, says the Lord, thoughts of peace, and not of evil, to give you a future and a hope. Then you will call upon Me and go and pray to Me, and I will listen to you. And you will seek me and find me, when you search for Me with all your heart. I will be found by you, says the Lord, and I will bring you back from your captivity; I will gather you from all the nations and from all the places I have driven you, says the Lord, and I will bring you to the place from which I cause you to be carried away captive."*
>
> *Jeremiah 29:11-14 NKJV*

Chapter 6

Hidden Idols

I DECIDED TO move on and make the best of my singleness. I didn't want to feel sorry for myself. That was just not me. I had no responsibility for anyone but myself, and had more time on my hands than a wife and a mother. I began to take some college classes for small business management and considered opening a hair salon. I exercised regularly and started piano lessons; one day I hoped to surprise my dad and show him I was worth having classes after all. I vacationed in the Caribbean with my girlfriends and got involved with as much as I could. I bought myself a Shitzu puppy for more companionship. I joined the Nursing Home Ministry and chose to be a blessing to others and get myself off my mind by simply staying busy.

I purposed to be okay with my life, whatever God's plan was. I was learning to put my selfishness aside and be thankful for the good things I had. I tried to be okay with the fact I was still alone and may be forever. I even talked to people as if I was fine with my singleness, but deep down it was still the cry of my heart to have a family of my own.

I prayed that one day I'd have a husband who had strong faith and would want to raise our kids with love and a great community of people. I had an ache in my soul as I would watch the little children singing or performing at church, experiencing a healthy and loving environment of which to belong. It was so different from my past and if God would only grant me the chance, I would raise my own like this and make my (Father) God proud too.

During this long period of time I made some progress, although I continued to struggle with my dad's decisions and his inability to connect with Yvette and me. It was difficult accepting that he wasn't making an effort to be the dad that the little girl inside me still longed for. I was tied emotionally in a way I couldn't shake completely. It only made me long to fill that disappointment with someone else to love and appreciate me. I asked God, *How do I know that you even care about this dream of mine, God? Do I dare ask you again for a sign? I just don't understand what I'm not doing right!* Over the next two years I dated men but nothing felt like marriage.

My friend Donna opened a beauty salon and offered me a chair to rent. A change in location and atmosphere was appealing after years of working in a noisy, busy mall. I needed change, hoping to get out of the rut I was in. I had a faithful following of clients which would keep me busy enough. Donna was also aware of some of my struggles in life which is why she loaned me the book that helped me about four years earlier.

Her wedding day had arrived and I again had nobody to join me as a date. I told her and my friends why I was not planning to go up to try to catch her bouquet, even if I was still single!

The moment came at her wedding for the bouquet toss. A few people at my table tried to force me up to the gathering of single girls. I grabbed my camera as I left my seat and walked over to the opposite side of the room, in front of Donna. *It would be a perfect picture,* I thought. She would be in the front of the picture, throwing her flowers over her head and the girls behind would be racing to catch it. As she threw the flowers in the air, I took a picture. I looked to see who caught it and there was a commotion and people looking and pointing in my direction. I looked around me, trying to figure out what they were saying. Donna screamed at me, "Look down!" The bouquet had landed at my feet! Surprised and baffled, I picked it up and asked,

"How did this happen?"

Donna laughed and yelled, "It hit the ceiling fan and it hit it back to you! This one was supposed to go to you this time!"

I later thought about the two different occasions with the bouquets and what they each represented. It was obvious there was a paradox. Perhaps God was trying to tell me something: *If I don't get ahead of God, striving eagerly to obtain my dreams out of fear and loneliness and disappointment of my past, I won't get hurt. That was symbolic of the first bouquet, with the bloody nose, the embarrassment and the emotional pain. The second bouquet that landed at my feet, by no action of my own, was simply a fluke when it hit the ceiling fan, sending it in my direction and at my feet. This paradox represented the trust I would need at that time, for God to bring my dreams to a reality. This happened in a way that could only be by His doing, not within my own or anyone else's control.*

I accepted this as a clear sign from God. How could it be otherwise? It made me think about the things I had been learning at the time. Did it also mean that I would be the next to be married? I had been making progress by accepting my life, and had stayed the course quite well. I was twenty-five years old, a good age to meet someone and start a family in a couple of years. Could the right one be right around the corner?

A sense of excitement and expectancy rose in me. It was not just coincidence that this happened. *Is my future husband attending my church and I don't yet know who he is?* I thought. There were some very nice men there that I considered to be more my friends. I was more attracted to a little more rough-around-the-edges type. I felt that my past would be more relatable to someone like that. I wanted someone who could appreciate the person I was for the mess I'd come through. I believed that someone coming from a sheltered Christian or educated background wouldn't understand, therefore I wouldn't feel as connected. If he could relate to the same need for God's help as I've had, that should be more promising for a meaningful connection.

Hidden Idols
Key Points

"The heart is deceitful above all things and desperately sick;
who can understand it?"
Jeremiah 17:9 ESV

Emotional Idols

An emotionally healed person is more apt to control their feelings, using them to advance their growth, not stifle it. They also advance the growth in others. Emotionally wounded people tend to allow their emotions too much influence, which can lead to draining others.

We've all had thoughts like, *If only I could have this thing, I would feel better*. Our emotions can be quite delusional. They are temporary and fleeting. They weave their way into our reasoning and then into irrational behavior. Unmet dreams can become idols. Focusing on what you don't have can have a darkening effect on the soul.

Idols are connected to our deepest emotions. Idolatry puts value on something or someone as a counterfeit for the perfect love our soul is thirsting for. If that perfect love has not been developed and experienced within, we have a tendency to try to fill that void our own way. Emotions are necessary but we are not supposed to be ruled by them. Making emotional decisions without adequate experience and logic can be detrimental.

Our emotions don't lie. There is a reason the need for the idol is so desperate. The hurt, which is associated with the longing, yearns for relief. The longing heart has never been able to grow into its essence because of inhibited emotional development. This is why some people fret over attaining the idol and may even sacrifice their integrity. The emotional longing sets into the belief system, then the person builds life on the faulty foundation. The reason we can't control feelings is that we are being controlled by our wounded soul.

We can't change what we don't understand. Our mental systems were formed in childhood while we were emotionally deprived and inadequately shepherded. Beliefs such as: *If only I had a perfect family, I wouldn't be this way*, or; *if only I felt valuable and cherished by my mom, dad or a certain person,* are difficult to reason with. Trusting in a loving authority may take some time to learn. In the meantime, we are internally incomplete and emotionally immature.

> *"For as he thinks within himself, so he is."*
> *Proverbs 23:7 NASB.*

Idols Drive us from the Outside In

> *"When I was a child, I spoke like a child; I thought like a child, I reasoned like a child. When I became a man I put away childish things."*
> *1 Corinthians 13:11 NASB*

Maladaptive thoughts started in childhood, weaved into our belief system and can be difficult to remove. We can be quite creative and *dress up* idolatry, fitting it right in to the cultural environment. I can relate. I became skilled at pretending I was just fine in order to keep my own lonely and empty reality intact. Some people know that their early wounds have something to do with why they don't feel free inside, yet are unaware of how to get free. Only knowing the truth can set them free. The longer the child within remains wounded or frozen, this unmet dream drives much of their actions and thoughts until further truth comes to light. Sanctification is a lifelong process.

> *"For I do not do the good I want to do, but the evil I do not want to do I keep on doing. Now if I do what I do not want to do, it is no longer I who do it, but it is sin living in me that does it."*
> *Romans 7:19-20 NIV*

In the context of relationships, feeling loved and valued is what we seek. To belong helps us deal with the pain, loneliness or insecurity we felt as a child. People can bring good things out in us but do not complete us. The union with someone does not *become* their identity. True freedom must happen on the inside through the healing and maturing of our true essence. Only then can you love out of the overflow within.

Seeking love, validation and identity through others may cause pressure on other people, and disappointment, leading to codependency. If you value certain goals more than your potential spouse, this may cause conflict in the future. Never assume they are *in it* with the same passion as you.

When people enter relationships as incomplete people, it's a matter of time before underlying issues come to the surface. Unmet dreams can make people do desperate things. Sometimes greater pain is what it takes to see the error of their thinking. Sadly the idols must be exposed for what they are. They are illusions of the truth and not a substitute for inner healing.

> *"Casting down imaginations, and every high thing that exalts itself against the knowledge of God and bringing into captivity every thought to the obedience of Christ."*
> *2 Corinthians 10:5 KJV*

Identity Idols

Our identity personifies what we value. Our life experiences, our purpose and all we consider most meaningful will shape our outward identity. A desire for significance, comfort and control can be desires driven by our ego, which to a point are not wrong. In fact, those goals help develop character and discipline. The danger is when those goals become deceptive baits, feeding the ego with pride, while our essence remains underdeveloped. We cannot become our authentic selves until we learn who we really are at the core, regardless of man's opinion of us.

Solomon and all his riches and success eventually saw everything as vanity. His words give us great wisdom about what's eternally important. We see the damage resulting from only having outward significance in some celebrities' lives. We see it in the lack of important virtues once held by healthy families, in our government and nation which seems to rather feed narcissism. People lose their true identity seeking the approval of man, while losing the attachment and approval of the Father of our essence.

"... for God sees not as a man sees, for man looks at the outward appearance, but the Lord looks at the heart."
1 Samuel 16:7 NASB

We all need to learn what it feels like to be fully known, or *spiritually naked*. It can seem easier to pretend that nobody knows who we really are; but God does. Those who have found their true identity in Christ experience His seed planted in their essence. As we are grafted into Him through the process of surrender and sanctification, we return to our true center, but only when we realize *who we are not* and *what will not satisfy*. This is where many Christians can get stuck as we easily get caught up in the pressures of an insecure identity. God allows us to fail in our own strength for our own good. The good news is, God never gives up on us.

"Indeed, my people have committed two evils: they have forsaken me, the fountain of living water, and have dug cisterns for themselves, broken cisterns, that can hold no water."
Jeremiah 2:13 ISV

As God's children, He wants nothing to get in the way of that intimacy with us. He is jealous of the broken cisterns we turn to, never delivering true satisfaction. There is transforming value when the pain teaches us we were deceived. By then we are more willing to be emptied in order to be truly filled. Jesus is that cup that won't run dry. Until then, the soil of our heart must be toiled for the seed to grow.

Chapter 7

The Incomplete Attraction

A FEW WEEKS later, a girlfriend named Linda and I attended a small concert in the Detroit area. Standing in the church lobby during an intermission with my friend, I felt a pair of hands cover my eyes from behind me. I couldn't guess who would be there. We didn't hear that anyone we knew was coming.

He removed his hands and there stood Scott with Carl. I knew Carl, and I had seen Scott around the church but really didn't know him. We joined them where they sat and watched the rest of the concert together. We had some small talk afterwards. On the way home I talked to Linda about Scott, and I decided he was a nice guy. Perhaps nice enough to get to know him better.

We talked a few times at gatherings at people's homes for fellowships. One day he came to the salon for a haircut and we went out for coffee afterwards. I learned more about him and I shared more about myself. He drove large transport trucks and had a secure job. He had just got out of a bad relationship and we talked about that. He had initially moved to Windsor to attend Brentwood Recovery Center and Carl, whom he worked with, invited him to Windsor Christian Fellowship. He'd been attending there just under a year. I found him attractive, with his slightly longer hair, strong build and a past with similarities to mine.

He talked about the day he and Carl ran into Linda and me at the concert in Detroit. He explained that weeks before, he wanted to get to know me better, seeing me around the church, but he wasn't sure how to make that connection with me. He had just been talking with Carl about how he felt drawn to me and even sensed I was to be his future wife. He asked Carl how he should make an attempt to get to know me. He said that he no sooner spoke this than they came around the corner to the lobby at that church, and there I stood with Linda. Carl responded, "Well Buddy, I think you have your answer!"

He told me, "At that point, God had confirmed that we need to be together."

I found it so interesting that this was going on for him. What were those odds? He spoke about the many times he would stand at the public telephone and watch for me at the salon just to get a glimpse of me. It was flattering to be put on such a pedestal! I saw him around the church but if anything I thought he avoided me or didn't really notice me. He told me that he was scared of me and that I might be too stuck-up for him. As I shared the real me, the one who lived on a farm, had a rough past and relied on God in my life, he said that drew him even more to me. He was intrigued by the things I did. He told me that he was now convinced that I was the one that God had for him. Perhaps all these coincidental events, including the bouquet, have a meaning?

I began to feel a sense of awe of all that was happening. It felt good to be the center of someone's world for a change. How could I not allow myself to be the recipient of such attention? He sent a huge flower arrangement to the salon where I worked. We took long drives and showed each other where we grew up. We saw each other almost every day. There were things I really liked about him. He could relate to my past struggles and seemed to understand the past I'd come from. He liked to talk a lot and there was never a dull or boring moment. I began to let my emotions experience the possibility of what this could mean.

There was a sense of neediness and insecurity that I was attracted to. I wanted to be needed. On the other hand there were times I was concerned about it. He often acted intensely when he had feelings about things. He definitely seemed in touch with his emotions—not like some men who never talk about them. In a strange way, I liked that side. He knew what he wanted and didn't hesitate stating it. In fact, when asked me to marry him, we stood in the middle of the road but I didn't get an answer out because we needed to get out of the way of traffic. I wasn't sure I was ready anyway.

As we walked downtown one day he led me into a jewelry store and showed me what he'd like to get me and quickly put the order in for the one I liked most to be sized. I remember thinking, *This is going too fast!*

A few weeks passed and I began to question my unrest. I told him that we should take it slower and not see each other as much. I decided not to sit with him at church and he sat on the opposite side. I could see him in the distance and felt I was upsetting the things he'd been experiencing. We went for a drive one day and I explained why I didn't feel good about the hesitance I had about our relationship. He became irritated and threw down the receipts for the ring order and said, "Well what are we going to tell them at the jewelry store?" Frustrated, I opened the car door, got out and began walking. He got out and went around the car and met me. I stepped aside, and he stepped aside as to teasingly play with me. I began to cry and he held me. I wanted all these feelings of confusion to just go away!

Over the next few days we talked and he explained that if I didn't marry him, he was going to move back to London. His time at Brentwood Substance Abuse Recovery Centre was finished and if I didn't marry him there was no reason for him to stay in Windsor.

My decision to slow down not only was disappointing to him but I could lose the possibility of soon having what could finally be the dream of marriage and family. Besides, time was ticking and if we would spend a year or two together before having a few kids, I would be approaching my thirties. *Was the bouquet tossed by the ceiling fan landing at my feet a sign from God? He was the person next in my life who was ironically pursuing me as such.*

I began to think, *Maybe I was being too critical of some of his recent displays of anger. I had been resenting the fact he made me get rid of my little dog because he didn't like him. I shouldn't expect perfection. I'd become quite picky so perhaps it was time to loosen up a bit. Isn't it necessary to have some faith in what we cannot see? Things don't have to be perfect. That takes time and love gives up the right to be right all the time. I could love him back to life in the areas he struggled. He just needs love and I've so badly wanted to give that to someone. He's had challenges related to being adopted and difficult challenges in childhood similar to mine. He just needs someone to love him the way he deserves. He wanted the same things in life as I did. We had the church community as support and we would send our kids to the Christian Academy there. We had God and a church family to help things along.* I began to let my defenses down. We began to plan the wedding of my dreams.

Ironically, that year, June 29th was a Saturday. It was my parents' anniversary date. I would use that date as a representation of a marriage that will stay together! It was a way to re-define all that was associated with a failed marriage and my painful past. This marriage was to define the future for my children and set the course for hopeful things to come. How fitting I thought that that wedding date would be. I shared those thoughts about the date with Scott. He seemed adamant that having the date close to both Valentine's and his birthday was more fitting. I don't remember why I didn't pursue my reasoning, but I obviously gave in to his. The date was set for February 16, 1991, only four months from our first date.

The wedding was beautiful, except that my dad didn't come because his wife was angry that I invited two of his former girlfriends. Everyone in the wedding party had stories to tell. Carl, who was Scott's best man, shared his story of the coincidental meeting with Linda and me at the concert in Michigan, after he'd just talked to him about how Scott should approach me at church someday. I took the opportunity to share my interpretation of the paradox of the Two Bridal Bouquets and what I believed God was saying to me about Scott. I told our guests about what I had learned from this ironic message:

> "At two different weddings, these bouquet tosses each
> meant something to me. With the first bouquet toss,
> I was hit in my face by the bouquet or someone's fist,

causing me pain—a representation of my loneliness and impatience while waiting on my dream marriage. After choosing to wait on God's promises, the second bouquet was different as it hit the ceiling fan then landed at my feet unknowingly. That strange occurrence signified to me that God fulfilled a promise to me in a miraculous way; when He orchestrated our coincidental meeting at the concert after Scott had just prayed about us getting together. These two ironic events were symbolic of the wind of God's direction. Therefore, the Lord had simply put it like this: By the wind of my Spirit I will bring my promises to you. The ironic and unexpected meeting the night at the concert had confirmed to me that God had brought him to me."

The Incomplete Attraction
Key Points

Insecurity Skews our Perception

It's human nature to crave intimacy. People with or without emotional deficits can experience the biochemical rush and emotional intoxication of newfound love. During this exhilaration, people with unhealed hurts seem to come alive with hope for the future as if their ship has finally come in. Without a balance of spiritual, emotional and physical intimacy, relationships lack depth and value and cannot offer true security through life's challenges.

Being in emotionally healthy love should not be something we imagine, fantasize or hope for, but it's something we know in our hearts is right. God believes more in us than we do in ourselves. In His perfect plan, things are not cloudy when making a life-changing decision like marriage. Knowing our true and secure identity sets us free to love the way God intended. We can recognize and experience a safe and balanced relationship. Entering one without such confidence is very risky. It's important to define what is driving the urgency. An underdeveloped core essence affects how we perceive right and wrong and how to manage impending dysfunction.

Recognize the Warning Signs in People

A person who has arrested development can put on a lot of faces and go through the motions with ease with their pseudo-personality. They can be very charming, hard-working, comical and may even come across quite emotionally intimate. Hidden motives such as fear of rejection can motivate a person to become skilled in seeking approval. Some may be able to put on their best face for years so you must keenly watch for authenticity. Even though they can be very alluring, there are signs to look for that may reveal a lack of emotional development or even a mental disorder. If you are not whole as an individual, you can easily ignore the signs that something's just not right. Here are a few warning signs you should never ignore:

- A lack of respect for your feelings, interests or values
- Not able to genuinely be sorry or take ownership where they've been wrong or insensitive
- Shifting blame on you
- Unusually quick emotional attachment
- Unstable temper
- Extreme jealousy or insecurity
- Aggressive body language
- Lack of self-restraint
- Addictive patterns
- Pressure for you to do things their way and minimizes your input
- Lacks empathy towards you and diminishes your feelings
- Condescending or intimidating treatment
- Angry when faced with opposition
- Pressuring you to have sex
- Frequent mood swings
- Often points out faults

- Demanding of your time/ expects you to do things that he can do
- Warnings from others
- Differing future goals; and passions about family/ministry future
- Lazy, lacking incentive or motivation
- Avoids or criticizes authority

A person who has most of these traits has a lot of emotional and spiritual growing to do. If someone goes to church and claims to *love God* there should be signs that follow. You have a right to inspect if there is good fruit coming from the tree. Do they have Christ-like character? Are they just going through the religious motions without an intimate relationship with God? Does he treat his mother and you with respect? Does he ask you what you think and feel about things? Do you share common foundations and goals for life? Does he have decent friends?

Matthew 7:17, paraphrased: a good tree bears good fruit. Underdeveloped trees that have a weak root system may not ride out the storms of life well. Bad fruit can lead to toxic relationships when it's not managed well by the pruner. There is more on this topic in the chapters following.

"If any of you lacks wisdom, you should ask God, who gives generously without finding fault and it will be given to you."
James 1:5 NIV

Chapter 8

Familiar Relationship Patterns

I GAVE BIRTH to Natasha only eleven months later. I was not careful to prevent such a quick pregnancy and Scott was willing to start a family right away anyhow. Starting a family early would only reduce any risks of problems in case time was against us. Strange logic perhaps but I still was thrilled that I even got pregnant since Scott was unsure if his past cocaine use would have lessened the chances to become a father.

She was a treasure to the both of us! I thought that she could only bring Scott and I closer to each other and make us more complete. I saw him one time gazing into her eyes with his tears flowing down his face. She gave us further reason to live respectable lives and raise her and our other children in a way they deserved. She was a very busy baby and kept me awake most nights. I was severely sleep deprived and fatigued. I never asked Scott to help at night, nor did he really care to.

Having his own child may have sparked an interest in learning more about Scott's birth parents. He was adopted at birth and taken in by parents who loved him and did their best. His mom had some painful issues from her past and turned to alcohol to numb life's stressors. Sadly, violating trauma came to him by way of a babysitter. He also learned at a tender young age that he was adopted. He felt unconnected but was told he was special.

He had struggles through his childhood and adolescence, trying to sort out the confusion inside. He spoke of a disconnect he had with his adoptive parents and said he was more connected to his grandfather and grandmother. When his parents didn't give him what he wanted, his grandparents would often come through for him. This was irritating to Fred, his dad, because this undermined his parental authority. He tried to teach Scott to earn things and work hard to get what you want.

Scott's desire to learn more about his lineage led him to hire a private investigator to find his birth mother. They found the family and suspected she had just recently moved to Florida. We were so close to finding her, but now that she moved away, it would be harder to meet her. When he sent her a video of us, we did not hear back from her. This perhaps deepened his feelings of rejection which seemed to come to the surface since he became a father to his own child.

I was able to stay home with Natasha and watch all of her first accomplishments. I selected clients that I would feel comfortable bringing into my makeshift in-home salon. I would do their hair while she was napping, or involve her with our guests if she wasn't.

Scott's inquisitive pull toward his Jewish roots had grown, and he wanted so badly to go to Israel with Pastor Rick and Cathy and about forty others. I really didn't want to leave Natasha behind, and I felt like I was abandoning her. I felt forced to accept this choice, regardless of how I felt. She would be in loving hands with Scott's sister and brother-in-law and their two children. I loved and respected that family.

It was an awesome experience walking in the streets where Jesus walked. Exploring the landmarks of stories made scripture come alive. One day while we were there, I had accidently left my credit card in a restroom. Scott became so irate with me at the huge inconvenience and risk of someone using the card. He would not let up on me no matter how sorry I was. He was even being verbally abusive to me around some of the ladies in the group, which surprised me that it didn't seem to bother him that others noticed. As he was walking angrily ahead of me, I watched him shaking his head and throwing his hands around in the air. I began to ponder the fact that this man isn't the person I married. Fear rose up inside me, as I felt disconnect and hurt. I married this person for life. What if this happens more frequently in the days ahead? Within one or two hours of backtracking to the restroom, the honest person that found the card returned it to me when we got there. Thank God! I thought I would never hear the end of it!

Around two years later we had our second daughter, Jericka. She was much less fussy as a baby and perhaps I was a much more relaxed mother the second time. She was much more content to hang with me unlike Natasha who had the world to discover.

The girls were so much fun. I loved being a mother. I even entertained thoughts of having another child right away and put my time and energy into little people who were receptive to my love. They were like sponges soaking up life's experiences with such excitement! They were so happy and full of personality. Everything was fun to them, making crafts and having story time. I captured hours of their childhood on video, wishing somehow I could freeze time in reality.

We loved to dance, jump and praise God together to children's music. At times the praise and words in these songs were like warfare in the heavenly realm against the Goliaths in life with words like: *hya hya, lift Jesus hya* and *thump, thump, Goliath!* They loved children's church, and all of their friends there. No matter what was happening in my marriage, I thanked God for the blessings then and for the future, believing that the chains of darkness were broken over my family.

We frequently visited his family in Bothwell and Petrolia Ontario. They loved to see the girls. They were very happy that Scott's life was going so much better since his past struggles before we were married.

Parts of my own life dreams were coming together. We had two beautiful daughters who were so precious to me and I had the privilege of being home with them full-time, which is what we'd agreed to do while they were not yet in school. This should have been one of the happiest times in my life as I imagined. Things just didn't feel the way they should by this point. Scott was easily irritated and his tone was very negative and cynical at times. His expressions and words were hurtful and very mean on certain days. He had many issues with his boss and people he would have to interact with at work. He would talk on the phone for hours with his friend Bill, about all of his misery in his life. He read newspapers and watched television for hours. I saw the parenting role becoming more my duty than sharing the work with him. In a way, I felt better as I subconsciously protected my daughters from any of his irritations.

I purposed to love him unconditionally, and praise him for any good I could see in him. I was committed to make this marriage work and I prayed that God would give me the grace to love him even when it was hard. As we learned in our pre-marriage classes I would do what Ephesians 5:3 said: wives, respect your husbands. I wouldn't try to change him but trust that God would work in his heart as I denied my own feelings. I never wanted to be seen as a nagging wife. I figured that an atmosphere of peace was more important. I believed that between me and God, love would heal his childhood pains relating to being adopted and other negative experiences.

Scott began to have an interest in large dogs and wanted to get a Rottweiler. One dog led to three large dogs that he refused to get spayed and neutered. Adding to the loads of work was a new network marketing opportunity, selling supplements. It took up much of my time and I felt forced into something I really didn't want to do, but he was convinced that the potential for greater wealth would be foolish not to put time and energy into. My in-home hair business kept me plenty busy.

The constantly hectic way of life caused me physical and mental exhaustion. It kept me from taking care of myself. If I had time and focus, I would have liked to educate myself about parenting and the difficulties arising in our home.

At times, I felt consumed with trying to help Scott through his issues. I wanted so badly for him to be free from his emotional state and from his negative thoughts, which for some reason he couldn't seem to control. I tried to encourage and inspire him through relevant articles or scriptures. At times he seemed to understand, and he would mellow out for a while. I wanted him to know that I was there for him and to be comforted at least with my commitment and understanding. I would give him no reason to be disappointed with me as his wife. I'd promised when I married him that I was committed and I made sure I satisfied his every need, even when I would be so exhausted at the end of the day.

The reality was clearer to me that there was unfinished business in Scott's life. He wasn't healed from emotional wounds from his past. I learned through this period in my life what it meant to deny myself, take up my cross and press on, as if one day I'd attain some prize. I chose to refrain from conflict about things; besides, he would get so intense when I shared my concern or opinions. I chose to be devoted to this marriage and God with a positive attitude. I resisted the feelings of anger and self-pity. I consciously focused on being thankful to God for all that was good. Listening to praise music helped sustain an attitude of praise and surrender in my heart to God. Seasons of grace helped me love him deeper and pray harder. Besides, I believed that God would someday show Scott that true satisfaction did not come from the outside but from within. I chose to do my part and set my mind on the bigger picture and be thankful for the promises in the future. I couldn't change Scott but I could change me. At least God would be pleased with my commitment to love, which I believed would not return void. One day soon, perhaps Scott would get his breakthrough. Loving him should make it all worthwhile!

Familiar Relationship Patterns
Key Points

"For you did not receive the spirit of slavery to fall back into fear, but you have received the spirit of adoption as sons, by whom we cry, Abba! Father!"
Romans 8:15 ESV

Blind Spots and Toxic Patterns

Trials interfere with our plans because there may be something we need to learn. Our own perceptions and beliefs can cause us to miss the wiser path to our own dreams. Even if we tried to avoid repeating our parents, we have similar functional patterns in adult life. Not that our outlets are wrong, but without divine grace and wisdom weaved into them, they are functioning modalities. Regardless of the outlet, darkness in the soul must be dealt with at the core and be revealed for what it is. In cases where the outlet is an asset like work or exercise; over time, that strength over-extended may become a weakness. In terms of the dysfunctional relationship, an imbalance in the roles can become a problem.

Within our relationships, we often have unconscious attraction to someone with a different face but familiar dynamics comparable to childhood emotional ties. It feels normal because that was what we knew. We don't know what we don't know, especially if we've never known healthy intimate relationships. These are blind spots and they continue into our adult relationships because the void for love was not satisfied as a child. Blind spots cause people to have a tendency to overlook a reality where others may not. If you don't learn about what your blind spots are, you could delay your personal growth for years because life seems comfortable, but it`s not necessarily healthy.

> *"Search me, O God, and know my heart! Try me and know my thoughts! And see if there be any grievous way in me, and lead me in the way everlasting!"*
> *Psalm 139:23-24 ESV*

Enmeshed Relationships

Most codependents lacked value as a youth, which often inhibits their discernment and ability to confront others about their behavior. This causes them to be enmeshed emotionally with the person they want to help while losing more of their own identity. Codependent people let the feelings and actions of others affect them to the point they lose control of their own lives and emotions. Many find that familiar place of silence and repression as a sense of help for the relationship. When there's a lack of emotional connection, many codependents make up for the lack of warmth and love in the home. They may compensate by over-nurturing their children in an effort to help the child feel secure in a home with the parent who isn't as caring or empathetic.

Children can be a somewhat satisfying and wondrous distraction from the lack of a meaningful connection within a marriage. Sadly, children take on those patterns of not trusting, not communicating and not feeling. Shutting down their emotions leads to a lack of experiencing mutually satisfying relationships. They too can become entangled by the needs of the parent and the dysfunctional cycle begins in another generation.

Be mindful of these ruts of familiarity. The comfort of the familiar keeps you from a freedom you've never known.

> *"We grow more spiritually from doing it wrong*
> *than from doing it right."*
> *Falling Upward by Richard Rohr*

Chapter 9

Adversity and the Lost Self

THE PHONE CALL could hopefully lead to some closure for Scott. It was Scott's birth-father Mark. Mark had recently found his other son, Ted, who was Scott's half-brother. Scott told Mark of his past attempt to contact his birth-mother, Lynne. Mark said that Lynne was the wrong one, that his birth mom was Lynne's sister, Marilyn, from Chatham. Perhaps after all these years of thinking she rejected him again, maybe she didn't reject his invitation by video to meet him after all.

Mark contacted Scott's real birth mother, Marilyn. He encouraged her to meet their son. She agreed to and they made a plan to all get together for a reunion. I became disappointed to hear that Marilyn did not want me around for their meeting the first time, even to take a video of the event. I was so happy for him and I loved the thought of sharing this moment with him! I chose to be supportive anyhow. As Scott left that day for the reunion I held his hand, looked into his eyes, hesitant to let go, knowing the days ahead were going to be different, as if further disconnect was coming. I sensed this may mean more to him than I was comfortable with. I wanted to be happy for him, yet I couldn't help feeling unsure about what was around the corner.

Natasha, Jericka and I decorated the house with balloons, streamers and words saying: *Happy Reunion Marilyn and Daddy!* It was a reason to celebrate. I hoped this event would lead to something special like we saw on the Oprah Winfrey Show, where everyone lived happily ever after. If things didn't feel like that, they both should know by seeing us celebrating with them that this is a family event that affects all of us. In preparing this celebration he shouldn't see my uneasiness about the way things were feeling to me. He had bought new clothes and insisted we buy new furniture since he wanted to give a good first impression.

I received a phone call from Scott's adopted mother, Gail. She and Fred had just met Marilyn as they had stopped on their way to Windsor. She wanted to warn me that Marilyn was quite clingy. I was already trying to fight the emotions inside but hearing that she was clingy bothered me even more.

Soon they came to the door and we all greeted one another. She had gifts for the girls and they were happy to meet their new grandma. I kept my smile pleasant and made a nice dinner. As I entered the living room with drinks for them I observed her sitting with Scott on the couch snuggled so close to him and caressing in ways that made me cringe inside. He seemed like he was soaking all this attention in. I pretended this didn't bother me and resisted the temptation to express my anger growing inside. I was never short of giving him affection so this shouldn't be something he needed from another woman.

I had prepared a bed for her to stay the weekend with us, since she lived in Ottawa and wouldn't be going home so soon, even though I wished she would. That didn't matter. She had planned to get a hotel room and stay there instead. Good, I thought. I couldn't wait for her to leave so that I could share my perspective of her with Scott. Soon, he drove her to her hotel and I was anxious for his return. The hours passed and it was late enough to get to bed. I tried to relax but my heart only raced as I watched the hours go by. Finally, at three o'clock in the morning he returned and I shared my thoughts with him. He agreed that she was quite clingy and he didn't notice just how close to his belt she was caressing. I hoped that by the next time with her he would be more aware and do something about it.

I didn't feel good about the interaction with her, even as I tried to make a connection. My sense was that she didn't want me around. *Was it insecurity or jealousy that I was experiencing?*

It wasn't her fault that they shared something so special that I couldn't be a part of. I longed for a deeper connection with Scott. I'd been working so hard to deserve that! It really began to feel like she was the other woman.

Scott and Marilyn would talk for hours on the phone. They would disappear for long drives. I prayed to God that, somehow, what I was seeing between them would be exposed as inappropriate and things would be put in the right perspective about their relationship. I was hoping that Scott would stand up for our marriage and respect my thoughts and feelings. Nothing was changing. He continued interacting with her just as much or more through letters and phone calls. He told me he was attempting to enlighten Marilyn to a Christian life, which I couldn't argue with. But I wanted closure for him to reconcile his past—not try to help her find something that she didn't seem to be interested in.

Marilyn paid for Scott to come and visit alone to their home in Ottawa. I practically begged him not to go, or at least to let me come too. It didn't matter what I felt, he decided to go alone regardless. He would get to meet her husband, and see their beautiful home. Again, I felt uneasy as he left, fearing even further distance from him.

Scott described their home as classy, professionally decorated and very high end. He was difficult to read and sort of shady about his visit when he returned home. Everything about this relationship just didn't seem to feel right to me.

"He fulfills the desires of those who fear him; he also hears their cry and saves them."
Psalm 145:19 ESV

Adversity and the Lost Self
Key Points

"One does not become enlightened by imagining figures of light, but by making the darkness conscious. The latter alternative, however, is extremely disagreeable and difficult and therefore very unpopular."
Carl Jung

Realizing our Own Misguided Maps

Life seldom works out the way we plan. Often, the challenges we face are the consequences of our own lack of wisdom and insight leading to feelings of despair, anger and more. It's a good time to evaluate what brought us to that place. Personal development takes moral courage to face those realities.

Marriage is one of the biggest platforms for us to discover our true selves and how to manage others wisely. Once the honeymoon is over, couples become less likely to try to impress one another. Children arrive and the self-sacrifice must really kick in during the sleepless nights, post-partum depression and the demands of life. Tension, irritability and the needs of others should expose the weaknesses in character and inspire couples to set goals to make marriage and family a success.

In order to make the home a safe haven for the growing family unit, there must be a plan to fireproof the marriage or couples lose sight of their oneness and personal growth. It requires a deeper look at how their goals of family success could be established and what to do with problems that arise. What an ideal character-building opportunity!

Within our relationships we will be faced with the reality of mankind's bent towards self-centeredness. Any issue that arises and brings on uncomfortable feelings require communication. Feelings should not be ignored or repressed. Remaining angry, stubborn, silent or unwilling to sacrifice, will not only stunt personal growth, but also attribute to dysfunctional relationships in the spouse and children. It's human nature to want control but if couples are equally determined to sacrifice their own desires at times, develop respectful and loving communication and pray together for direction, there is hope. Trials should be seen as bridges to cross to another level of wisdom, experience and intimacy which can lead to evaluate our core beliefs that are at the base of our emotions. They are opportunities to renew our minds in a higher truth and find strength to love as Christ did.

If ever you need God's grace, a challenging marriage would be the place. A commitment until death in marriage is a big one. It is also important to keep sacred your union with a God who wants to see you through these battles.

*"For I am confident of this very thing, that He who began a
good work in you will perfect it until the day of Jesus Christ."*
Philippians 1:6 NASB

Surrender, Grace and Sanctification

Grace is often thought of as mercy, favor or loving-kindness. It is those things but, on a spiritual level, it is a function of the purifying process at the core of our being, our essence, spirit and heart. It's the exchange of our incompleteness for His completeness. I almost titled this book *Empowering Surrender* for this very reason, but I wasn't sure people would be drawn to that oxymoron. Nonetheless, it takes surrender to access divine strength to overcome and become empowered. There is no other way to attain freedom from sin and darkness.

Christ personified love, but because we are sinners, we are only able to personify His love through the pure function of His grace. His love cannot originate out of our own righteousness because carnal love is tainted with sin. The grace to love (as He leads) can only come by the power to obey His Spirit in us. But first, our ego and will must be aligned with the function of grace. Carnal reasoning often has issues with this concept because of the need to have full control. Grace only operates through an intimate, childlike connection with a Holy God and Father. God's fullness can only come through our emptiness.

*"For it is by grace you have been saved, through faith—and
this is not from yourselves, it is the gift of God, not of works
so that no one can boast. For we are His handiwork, created in
Christ Jesus to do good works, which God prepared in advance
for us to do so."*
Ephesians 2:8-10 NIV

As I mentioned earlier, wounded does not mean broken. Many are wounded yet not broken. Broken is beneficial when it brings a person to the point of a healthy reliance and surrender. The point of surrender is probably the most powerful phase to be in spiritually. We are caught between a rock and a hard place and there is no way forward except to ask God for help. Just as in a healthy childhood relationship with a trusted parent, we run home where it's safe and ask for guidance. Brokenness leads to surrender, which leads to divine empowerment, which is grace. Our faith then has a chance to grow because it is all we have left to rely on to overcome our desperate situation. It forces us to abandon our control and surrender to a power greater than our own. That is very difficult for someone who has not yet learned to trust in an invisible God, much less in other people, but life's battles leave no wise alternative if we want to live within our essence. The sacrifice of your own control may just be a blessing in disguise! This blessing does not come easy. Being humble enough to ask God for help contributes to your spiritual growth, allowing for His grace to abound in your soul and hang on in faith. This is how your spiritual essence grows in you. Without the holiness of grace, intellectual *goodness* still leaves your core essence hungry for inner strength from the Father who designed it. In fact intellectual goodness can get in the way because pride can drive it.

"From His fullness we have all received grace upon grace."
John 1:16 ESV

Grace was a gift at salvation and continues to be accessible in the process of spiritual transformation from one moment of surrender to the next. Salvation is the first step, but we work out our salvation every time we face adversity, guided by the Father's will. Working with this process is called sanctification and renewing the mind according to scripture. It's a refining process which purifies us from the effects of sin and selfishness, which caused alienation from God in the beginning. Each challenge is meant to bring us to a point where we choose to do what's right and surrender the rest into the hands of the Almighty. Many people reject and resist the function of grace and sanctification in their lives. The need for control is greater than their need to surrender. As you read on in the story, you will see what I mean.

"I am speaking in human terms because of the weakness of your flesh. For just as you presented your members as slaves to impurity and to lawlessness, so now present your members as slaves to righteousness, resulting in sanctification."
Romans 6:19 NASB

Imperfect people have a great advantage if they are willing to look within and consider what they need to change. Pain fuels the soul, causing a search for relief. They have more opportunities to be pressed harder to accept that they need to change and may be more likely to surrender to God and seek His guidance to walk the wiser path. People who had more fortunate and comfortable upbringings may not be forced into a necessity to accept a higher truth. Grace is the restoration of the presence of God through the incarnate work of the Holy Spirit and our surrender to His leadings. A good acrostic for G-R-A-C-E is:

G—God's
R—Riches
A—At
C—Christ's
E—Expense.

"My grace is sufficient for you; for my power is made perfect in weakness."
2 Corinthians 12:9 NIV

Chapter 10

Redefining the Past

SCOTT WOULD HIDE in the bedroom or upstairs to talk on the phone. Why did he have to be so secretive if he had nothing to hide? I tried to listen for any more clues to get some clarity about this strange behavior.

After a few months, another surprise came to both Marilyn and Scott. Her birth daughter Mary was also given up for adoption, searched and found her birth mother, Marilyn. She was a half-sister to Scott, just a couple years younger and very pretty. She definitely looked related to both Marilyn and Scott. Mary and her husband Rick were very pleasant. I was hopeful that this new union would affect the course of the relationship between Marilyn and Scott. Anything at this point would have been a refreshing break for me.

On one visit to London without me, Scott, Marilyn and Mary stayed in a hotel room together, which I was uncomfortable about, but Scott did so regardless. Late that evening, feeling so hopeless and alone, I began to cry out to God. As I sat looking out the window, there was that familiar haunting childhood sadness again. The same scenario: the wind was blowing, and the trees were fiercely blowing during tornado warnings that night. There arose again in my soul the fear of the future regarding my precious and sacred family. It was that eerie reminiscence of the time when I cried out when I was young as my parents fought.

Only you know my pain and fear right now, God, so I'm laying them down at your feet so I can get your help! I'm so desperate inside I can't stand this! I began to imagine God holding me as a child, comforting me as I cried my heart out to Him to take the ache from my heart.

Suddenly in the midst of the consoling connection with God, I felt a deep buzzing and flutter right in my face. I screeched and saw this two-inch long, ugly black bug that I'd never seen before. All nerved up, I angrily killed it and reduced it to shreds while thinking, *How dare you Satan!* It had interrupted a time that I finally felt so abandoned to God. It could only represent the evil, dark and sinister work of Satan himself! I used the intense emotions and put them to good use as I knew then it was time to take charge. Instead of crying over this, I began to scream at him and prayed with authority on behalf of my husband and my cherished family. I realized the spiritual warfare at work. I spiritually took charge in that moment over every dark and sinister spirit that was prevailing. I screamed, "Get your hands off my family, Satan! I'm taking back my family and I'm standing on the promises of God and break every curse of darkness in Jesus name!" The evil influence and smashed black bug were symbolic of the curse over my marriage and our family. I would remember this moment and believed I would find out later what I was praying for and what changed on this very night.

Ironically things did begin to change after that night. Scott began to show irritation with Marilyn. There was a lot of *she said that he said* kind of tattling and talking behind each other's back when Mary came in the picture. He began to be intensely angry with his words toward Marilyn and she became quite defensive back at him. This would draw such a rage from within him, I couldn't believe the intensity. He commanded her to be truthful as she twisted stories to suit her side, apparently. As selfish it was of me, I was happy he was feeling that way toward her. At least there was finally a breakthrough!

At that point it began to feel like darkness was losing the battle. Scott didn't want Marilyn around anymore and he returned all the gifts she had given. She also returned those given to her, even the pictures. I was happy things had ended between them, but I became concerned about his emotionally cruel and rash treatment of her over what he said were lies. I had an idea there was more to the story than what I was hearing.

A few months later, after another screaming match on the phone with Marilyn, Scott hung up angrily. I sat with him like I often did, to get him to open up about whatever was disturbing him at that time. I said to him, "Scott, you have to move forward. Don't let this destroy you!" I then remembered my prayer to God that, whatever was hidden from me, I had a right to know about it, and that it would be revealed to me. I felt a strong prompting inside to hold his hand and say these words, "Scott, you would feel so much better if you would open up and be honest with me, about everything, even what went on between you and Marilyn. I know things happened between you two, but for you to be free, you have to tell me the truth. I promise to stand by you, no matter what. I already forgive you. Let's move forward, past all of this, and put this all behind, and start all over."

I was surprised that he began to open up to me, but God must have known he was going to. He began to tell me how the relationship crossed the marital lines with Marilyn and the various occasions when things happened between them. I got up from my seat and we held each other. I had so much happening inside my mind and body. Shocked, betrayed and violated, I tried to put in order what to feel first. I made the promise to be there for him and so for I knew I would. I wanted to say to him, "How could you?" But I wouldn't, at least not yet. I remained calm and gave him no reason not to continue with any more details. I wanted to know all of it. I had no reason to give up on our marriage, especially now that things had gone bad between Scott and the "other woman," Marilyn. I had him all to myself now, and even better, he was being honest, which made us feel more connected. He even agreed to get some marriage counseling, finally. What would stand in the way from things getting better from here forward? I had learned forgiveness before and I would forgive again, with God's help; this could be the beginning of better things to come. Besides, perhaps finally this would bring healing for both of us and closure from this ugly chapter in our lives.

At the weekly women's Bible study led by Margie Paolini, I shared with the ladies what I had learned about Scott and his birth mother that week. I was finally able to release some of the bottled-up horror I was feeling inside. The ladies lovingly prayed for me and encouraged me.

The betrayal felt worse than words could describe. The very thing I feared—losing the sacredness of our marriage—had happened. My dream since childhood turned into my nightmare. My marriage was supposed to be the one that others' wanted in their lives. I fought visions of their encounters they had together. *Why did this happen to my marriage, God? How could You allow this to happen to me and my children, of all people?*

I couldn't eat or sleep for days. Everyday tasks were challenging. I even had to focus on breathing right. I would replay the visions in my head of the times they were away together. I cried for hours, using the times alone so that my daughters wouldn't catch me in a bad state. I had to get past this, so that I would not give into being angry at Scott. I would give him no reason to not move forward and to put all of the pain and mistakes behind us. We did still have the future. He could grow into the man I thought I'd married.

The days that followed, Scott walked around with a sort of blank, sad stare and would cry easily. I played ministering music that sang of God's mercy and love for Scott, so that he would experience all of the love, forgiveness and hope for all that God had for him. It helped me to stay focused on the future as well. I rarely expressed my real pain to him or expose my own need for comfort. He knew it hurt me but he also knew I had purposed and promised to forgive him. I did everything possible to give our marriage a chance. I wanted to make sure he had all that he needed to move forward in this healing process, finally facing the childhood roots of rejection he had felt and the deceptive lie—that meeting his real mom would make everything better. All he needed to do was accept the love and mercy from both God and myself. Healing could flow into the deepest parts of his soul. I told him that his heavenly Father loved him more than any parent could have. He could finally learn what it meant to be adopted by His loving Abba Father and experience his spiritual inheritance of true security and perfect love. Life had to work out this way to heal the deep wounds of rejection, confusion and pain. This would bring closure. He would no longer need a mask to hide behind, nor deal with the pressures of acting in the false person just to belong. From this point forward he would know his true value and grow, safely.

I pictured all of the blessings that could come from all of the previous ugliness of this nightmare. I was ready to grow our marriage together into all that it was supposed to be. We would finally be best friends, open, honest and real. Some of these moments, we were closer to each other than ever before. The hope of good things to come from this horrible tragedy only seemed to make our love stronger. Though I had terrible grief, I had immense relief and hope for the days ahead. I chose to look ahead and not behind. I chose to see him as the man God created him to be.

"Let us then with confidence draw near to the throne of grace,
that we may receive mercy and find grace to
help in time of need."
Hebrews 4:16 ESV

Redefining the Past
Key Points

"The significant problems we face cannot be solved at the same
level of thinking we were at when we created them."
Einstein

Bearing the Pain of Poor Choices

Truth revealed can begin the process of living free from a lie. This is a moment where many people have finally hit bottom, facing the reality of their true condition because denial, deception and unhealthy patterns held them captive for years. Their own mental maps have led them off course. That reality stares them in the face. What they thought would work hasn't. People must learn how their earlier maladaptive beliefs led them down a deceptive path. Now it's time to make significant, life-changing choices and face some facts. The obvious fork in the road can be a costly one for them and the people closest to them. One way leads to spiritual transformation as seeds of faith can grow in softened soil. The other way leads to greater bondage and pain.

The Roles of Intimate Betrayal

The Betrayed Victim

Intimate betrayal strikes at the core of who we are; we are meant to be cherished, not forsaken, in marriage. Those who selflessly loved their spouse and deeply valued the sanctity of this sacred vow feel anguish in their soul. Sadly, their love was taken for granted but Jesus understands such betrayal. His desire is for the rescuer to know just how valuable he or she is to Him.

Showing grace, forgiveness and love in the face of one's own pain and loss does not mean that such a person is fearful, though many may assume so. The victim cares enough to love their mate through the pain to endure what's ahead for restoration. The person betrayed might repress their pain in order to keep their goal of a happy family intact and believe in a positive outcome. Instead of continuing to act as a nurturing mother, she needs to learn to be a wife. This is difficult for those who have a lower self-regard.

The violator may not even realize the depth of hurt they induced, especially while the nurturing victim doesn't adequately speak about their own pain. Therefore the offender continues to not fully understand the severity of the damage caused. If people are allowed to be human, realistically there should be an expectation of another's grief as a legitimate consequence. Empathy and ownership are good virtues for the violator to learn if the relationship is to grow. This is where a third party should be involved such as a therapist. There is so much that needs to come to the table on both sides of the intimate betrayal.

The Offender/Violator

Some people use relationships as they would substances without realizing the similar functioning dynamics. For this reason, the same type of accountability should be in place. The offender is faced with the reality of their impulsive condition. People with a history of addictions say this was their turning point when they accept their powerlessness over their addiction. Ownership of their actions is unfamiliar territory because having control was more comfortable and predictable over the years. The person lacking impulse control must be intentional about changing because continuing on the road of denial leads to further defeat. If they are teachable the problem is fixable.

Rebellion and Shame or Surrender and Guilt?

There are distinct differences between guilt and shame. Shame says, "I am bad or wrong," while guilt says, "I did something bad or wrong." It is so important to grasp this truth. Satan uses shame and condemnation, while God uses guilt, conviction, surrender and forgiveness. Satan uses denial while God uses confession.

Our true essence is not our behavior. The *false self* uses behavior and coping strategies. Our self-focused behavior leads us to succumb to our familiar ways in order to deal with what is hurting inside. Those behaviors require accountability, compliance and trust to recover the lost and wounded essence. People will either surrender to, or resist, the process of transformation that God allows for our eternal good.

> *"But each person is tempted when he is lured and enticed by his own desire."*
> James 1:14 ESV

Surrendering in the Process to
Recover the Essence

In an atmosphere of love, forgiveness and grace, healing is more accomplishable, just as a perfect parent guides a child with love and accountability. Their true essence is fed the nutritious food and living water which satisfies the thirsting soul (John 4:14). In doing so, the underdeveloped child within can safely unmask, address the sources of pain and give it a new meaning. Instead of subconsciously protecting their fearful core, they become open to learn and trust. After realizing they are guilty of using their carnal ways of control, children and adults can learn to change negative patterns and begin to build a safer relationship. They are recovering and maturing their true essence again. The brain begins to function as God created it by building new neural pathways based on the truth: their new reality. This improves the flow of serotonin, norepinephrine and dopamine, which naturally allows for better judgment and reasoning. This literally brings the inner child back to life, recovering their lost essence which sin had a hold of.

"Bless the LORD, O my soul, and forget not all his benefits, who forgives all your iniquity, who heals all your diseases, who redeems your life from the pit, who crowns you with steadfast love and mercy, who satisfies you with good so that your youth is renewed like the eagles."
Psalm 103: 2-6 ESV

Surrendering to the process of healing welcomes authentic relationships and deeper insight. This person can be a great help to others in crisis, which gives them a sense of purpose. Their recovered identity gives them a much better chance to succeed in every area. Addiction Support Groups are great to maintain acceptance and accountability. In many cases ongoing therapy is necessary. Trustworthy accountability partners are crucial and emotions must be regularly examined or else this narrow path to healing will not be an easy one.

"Confess your faults one to another. And pray for one another, that ye may be healed. The effectual fervent prayer of a

righteous man availeth much."
James 5:16 KJV

"A man's heart deviseth his way, but the
Lord directeth his steps."
Proverbs 16:9 KJV

Rebelling against the process of emotional growth leads to the decline of one's true essence and the relationships they have. People resisting ownership of their selfish behavior may function through denial, a defense mechanism. Without surrendering, the underdeveloped child within will try to keep their pseudo-personality intact. Their false self has created a system in order to cope within their environment. The façade used for protection is still more familiar, and has sufficed for many years. The brain has been conditioned this way and has lived more on self-protecting adrenaline instead of the wise judgement and concern for others.

If you remain in a relationship with this person, you may begin to sense emotional resistance and distance from them. They may use emotional manipulation if the weaker person tries to gain strength or place accountability on their resistant behavior. Deep down they don't like who they are so they avoid their own reality. They often shift blame and project it on others because they are relapsing back into their pseudo-personality. This façade uses their familiar defense mechanisms such as control, intimidation and attempts to weaken the identities of others. They cannot be their true self and may even forget who they really are at their core since they abandoned the child within. They don't like being vulnerable or not having control because they feel safer disassociating their true essence.

Without the jammed up emotions being released, they cannot experience true freedom and deeper connections with people. Grace cannot operate through them because they have not fully surrendered their control. Their personalities, interests and friends were fashioned through who they pretended to be. No wonder people are so reluctant to let go of their façades!

Hurting-people can hurt people, even the ones that love them the most. Even God won't barge down the door of their heart. Likewise, the people who are in their lives have little to work with and need to take care of their own emotional lives and be safe. The pain and disappointment however, is understood by Jesus, who was also despised and rejected of men. The darkest emotions of mankind can be brought into the light and healed. Refuse to give up hope, but learn wise ways to manage such relationship dynamics as these.

"And the light shineth in darkness; and the darkness comprehended it not."
John 1:5 KJV

Chapter 11

The Real You is God's Design

SCOTT AGREED TO go for marriage counseling, which went on for a couple of months. The counselor was a timid little lady and was hardly ever in control of the sessions. He talked most of the time about the surface issues unrelated to our deeper problem and how Marilyn and others had done him wrong.

We had also signed up also for a "Marriage Weekend" through our church. Maybe something good would light the flame that for some reason had started to dwindle. During our free time on the Marriage Weekend, we did some shopping. In a clothing store, he recognized a woman whom he'd known from his past. They talked about some other members of her family and I felt uneasy about their conversation as he seemed shady and secretive with her. I often second-guessed my insecure emotions, so maybe I was just still raw from everything.

The next morning, he arose early and I awoke to him looking through the phone book. He told me he was running out to get coffee. Suspicion rose up in me as he walked out. The hotel room had a coffee maker so that was not really why he left. Whatever address or phone number he was looking for, perhaps he was now out to find.

During the rest of the Marriage Weekend it was as if Scott was not even there. I was in a room of about fifty people and felt so desperately alone and—even worse—disconnected from the man I wanted to love me and care about what I was feeling, so that we could put our marriage back together. The closeness we had been feeling with each other was diminishing. He was withdrawing himself from me emotionally and even physically, disregarding and belittling me further.

Over the next few months, I saw in him a strong interest for purchasing a Harley Davidson. This seemed to be all-consuming and distracting from the previous months' tribulation. He'd been buying cases of beer more often. He attained a Firearms Acquisition Certificate, so that he could purchase a gun. His interest in these things seemed to replace the process of healing from what had surfaced.

Lately, he'd been acting so strange. He wasn't sleeping with me. He had me record some of my Christian music which he never really listened to. He would go for long bicycle rides, and claimed that the medication the doctor gave him made him feel different.

Another day, I mentioned my concern about our relationship and suggested we get back in for more counseling. He remarked with a snarl about how psychological I get about things. As I calmly explained that I just wanted to connect with him, he became very angry and said, "Get off of my case!" His rash treatment snowballed into calling me names and mocking me. *That did it! I've been silent and hurting for too long! I can't take this anymore,* I thought to myself. I felt myself begin to cave under the feelings of anger and betrayal again. Something in me just had to be expressed that very moment. I felt a rush through my mind and body as I looked for something to throw. I grabbed the first thing I saw, the remote control from the table, and threw it at him. He came at me and punched me in the face and we scuffled as the chair tipped backward.

Thankfully, the girls were asleep and didn't witness anything. I ran barefoot outside to avoid escalating the fight. I ran toward the dark woods outside of the neighborhood to cry out loud the rage and grief that was in me. Somehow the darkness and cold felt like a release in itself as I lay on the grass. After about an hour, I came back and went into the bathroom to check my fat lip. I came downstairs calmly to apologize and talk. I sat myself next to him and said, "I feel like our marriage is failing and you are acting like you're not even my husband anymore. I feel so alone and it's like you don't want to work with me to help our marriage work." I tried to get something out of him hoping to reach him. He was silent and unresponsive. I said, "If there is someone else, please tell me and stop hiding it! At least let me move on with my life if it's over!" I cried as if it already were over. There was still no response and his countenance was cold and distant.

At this point I had given all I could; I'd poured into the relationship all I had left, feeling still desperate to give something to make a change, but there was just nothing left to give. *God, I just need and answer. What is going on with him?*

A day or two after, as I was in the garage, I noticed some broken pieces of ceramic on the floor. As I studied it, it looked familiar. I went through the garbage and found more of the pieces. It was a figurine my mom had made when she did ceramics. At about ages six and eight, she asked Yvette and I to choose our dress colors, and she would paint Yvette's girl with the brown hair, and mine with blonde, and our names at the bottom. Why was it in the garbage if it had been in a safe place in Natasha's carpeted bedroom on a shelf? It was a figurine I cherished. I asked about it and Scott said he bumped it and it fell on the floor. It felt to me like the figurine represented the real me, how I was being shattered to pieces. Along with his emotional distance, this further confirmed my feelings that there may be a death wish over me. Strange and even sinister, I thought, especially after his strange behavior. It seemed symbolic of how I thought about my life and purpose. My life was shattered and so was I. I took the time to collect every piece and glued it all back together. I cried as I felt God say to me, *You may be broken, but I am re-creating you the way I designed you to be.* I decided that I would keep this recovered and restored figurine as a memory of this time in my life. One day it would all make sense.

It was hard to decide what to do next. There was obviously something that interrupted the plan of healing and restoration in our marriage. I knew that there was nothing more required of me as I have kept my heart as pure as possible, willing to make it work if Scott would only try. I desperately begged God to show me what to do from here since He is the only one who sees the big picture. The pain was getting too hard to bear. I needed some kind of answers or direction from God as to what to do. I was at the edge of feeling forsaken by God Himself, as I knew that He knew what this marriage meant to me. I clung to the tiny seed of faith that He would one day soon make things clear.

> *"The Lord Himself goes before you, and will be with you; He will never leave you, nor forsake you. Do not be afraid, do not be discouraged."*
> *Deuteronomy 31:8 NIV*

I was fortunate to have a few close friends to talk to and vent my feelings to. I met my friends Lynn Masse and Denise Bardsley for our routine walks around the church after our kids were dropped off at school. It was a great way to get exercise and catch up on all that was happening and pray for one another. I told them about the recent strange behavior Scott was displaying and how I felt he just didn't seem to want me anymore; in fact I sensed he could care less if I was dead. I told them about the ceramic figurine that strangely broke and how it was like the destruction and fragments from my whole life. I explained that it felt like an attack against my soul, body and even my future. Lynn said she thought that we should pray for my safety, and to break any curse or death wish against me, and so they did pray. I was now *covered by the blood of Jesus and no weapon formed against me would prosper, and that any curse against me would not prosper but be returned to those who sent it.*

That weekend, Scott heard of a tragic death in Bothwell. It was the brother of the woman named Laurie who broke his heart when Scott was sixteen years old. Scott would have to go to his funeral, but didn't want me to go along with him. He'd spoken about her in the past. He told me earlier that she was his first love. He told me they recently ran into each other in an elevator in Wallaceburg. Maybe it's her that he's seeing? He was making such a fuss about looking good and bought a brand new suit, shoes, shirt and tie for the funeral. This reminded me of when we had to refurnish and redecorate the house before Marilyn would come. *Hmm. God, show me again, please. I deserve to know what is hidden, just like you did before.*

The Real You is God's Design
Key Points

*"But now O Lord, thou art our father, we are the clay, and
thou our potter, and we all are the work of thy hand."*
Isaiah 64:8 KJV

Who am I Really?

We cannot escape who we really are. We are not always the person others see us as. We are not always who *we* think we are. Who we really are will eventually become evident. God sees us differently than people do. He holds the best version of our worthy, fulfilled and authentic self. He wants us living out our inheritance, blossoming, at peace and confidently full of God`s love so that nothing hinders our growth. We must be willing to see ourselves as He does. This can only happen when we are ready to deal with our false identity built on the wrong foundation. It may not seem false to us because it's all we knew. Parts of it were formed from the lack of perfect love, which all imperfect parents could not supply. Logically, everyone has a foundation worth rebuilding. Adversity in life gives us that opportunity, yet few embrace it to capacity.

*"I will give you a new heart and put a new spirit in you; I will
remove from you your heart of stone and
give you a heart of flesh."*
Ezekiel 36:26-27.

Are You Teachable?

Shattered dreams and broken pieces of our hearts give our loving God something to work with, but only if we let Him. Pain was our enemy but now it can be our ally. It can motivate us to look at how we got into difficult situations. The reality finally stares us in the face: that we may have been off course. The good part is that it reveals the idols we have unhealthy attachments to, and shows us that they will not bring us true satisfaction. Shattered dreams force us to change our limited carnal perceptions of life, making us more willing to accept higher ones. This is when the words of Christ really begin to make sense. When life falls apart, pain and healing can finally come together. It's time to get real about God, our choices and true intimacy with Him.

> *"For I reckon that the sufferings of this present time are not*
> *worthy to be compared with the glory*
> *which shall be revealed in us."*
> *Romans 8:18 KJV*

The Potter and the Clay

Consider yourself as clay and God as the Potter. He shapes and even crushes the stubborn, hard and atrophied pieces so that we are moldable in His hands. In the heat we are purified and refined. The end results are vessels of honor and trophies of His grace. If you're broken and shattered, willing to be molded by faith in His design, His grace enables you to cooperate with His plan. We've been given the power to endure the challenges that can lead to wholeness and purity of heart, just as Christ operated in. Divine strength will help you withstand adversity as you become internally strong. Through the process, He exchanges His beauty for your ashes. Ashes signify death of our old ways of control and maladaptive mental processes. The beauty signifies the grace and purity that comes through an empowering surrender. Our true essence is formed in the midst of the fiery trials of the refining process. We shed the useless ways of managing life and grow up stronger and live out His truth in our earthen vessels.

> *"And the God of all grace, who called you to his eternal glory in*
> *Christ, after you have suffered a little while, will himself restore*
> *you and make you strong, firm and steadfast."*
> *1 Peter 5:10 NIV*

The Most Secure Foundation

"And everyone who hears these words of mine and
does not do them will be like a foolish man who built
his house on the sand."
Matthew 7:26 ESV

For the person seeking God's will, every adversity has purpose. No trial is wasted. For many of us, there is no other way to reach the true and injured essence within. When we were wounded as a child and nobody helped us understand what was going on inside our heart and soul, Jesus was there. We just didn't know He was. We weren't taught that these times He would show us the way through life's storms. In our own strength we survived, alone, which made us carnally strong yet stubborn, guarded and perhaps even proud. God wants us to go back to that memory and see Him there, this time taking us by the hand, loving us and guiding us into His realm of safety and truth.

Through these challenging times, the mustard seed of faith can grow. Your trust in God's perfect love will build your foundation stronger than it was before. It becomes laced with a divine love for others. As He helps restore the pure essence that was lost through the darkness of deception, through the light of faith you'll see purpose in the pain. The old memories and neural pathways in the brain were making it difficult to allow this truth because it was too busy surviving on adrenaline protecting the childhood wounds. But now, the present battle takes on new meaning. There is no better choice but to accept this most healthy and logical truth.

Opening your spiritual eyes helps you to see that His plan has greater purpose than your present comfort. Everything that was built on the wrong foundation must be broken down and cut off. Those lies get in the way of God's plan, hindering the function of His grace in you. Scientifically speaking, this new reality slowly restores the flow of the brain's chemicals allowing you to trust again, leading you to be gently guided by God. Slowly, you gain more sensitivity to His voice. This is the manifest power of grace at work, restoring to the brain what was lost because of sin. Fear no longer has its place as perfect love replaces it. The fear foundation must be shaken and tore down, so that a faith-filled and secure foundation can be built on perfect love.

> *"For thus sayeth the Lord of hosts, once more in a while all that can be shaken will be shaken...The latter glory of this house will be greater than the former."*
> *Haggai 2:6-9 Paraphrased.*

Did fear or pride become a part of your foundation? Did you have to earn by way of your own efforts and works to attain love? These foundations will be shaken because they cannot handle adversity or create perfection and purity. Christ in us provides the grace to obey God, not by fear, but through love. Following laws and rules without grace always leads to emptiness because we are imperfect within ourselves. We cannot conjure up holiness and purity of heart. That's an inside job done by a holy God as we allow. We simply cannot be perfected in our essence outside of Christ's atoning work of grace. God is making a new foundation not built with our own hands, but by His spirit who dwells within you.

> *"For we know that when this earthly tent we live in is taken down (that is, when we die and leave this earthly body), we will have a house in heaven, an eternal body made for us by God himself and not by human hands."*
> *2 Corinthians 5:1 NLT*

There are times when there seems to be no answers when we ask, Why God? I know God could fix this. Why doesn't He? Where is His justice? When will He intervene? It's easy to just give up. Discouragement leads to unbelief which will only hinder your growth and cause a wedge in your relationship with Him. No matter how ugly things get, never turn your back on Him. Don't let discouragement bring you to the pit of despair. Continue to do what's right just as Christ stayed focused and connected to the Father through the toughest times. God knows what you feel and there are things going on behind the scenes in a spiritual war against your soul and your future. It's then you must hold on to Jesus with all of your might and never give up hope because heaven is warring on your behalf. He always has your best interest at heart in the end. Avoid any false reasoning that turns your heart away from Him. Put all negative thoughts captive to the truth (2 Corinthians 10:5).

"But those who wait for the Lord shall renew their strength,
they shall mount up with wings like eagles, they shall run and
not be weary, they shall walk and not faint."
Isaiah 40:31 NRSV

It takes time and intention to develop an eternal perspective. Examine your heart daily, pray and renew your mind with life-giving scripture. Uncovering the darkness will help us discover the healing power of God's light. You, with God, determine your future. Some of us have to learn these hard truths for ourselves, on our own terms, often leading to compromise, regret and pain. Our heavenly Father always extends His agape love, without conditions, offering immediate restoration when we finally come home to Him. When you do, there is nothing that can stop His purposes for your life to be unveiled in His timing. He's in the process of removing the obstacles between you and Him.

"You intended to harm me but God intended it for good to
accomplish what is now being done, the saving of many lives."
Genesis 50:20 NIV

Chapter 12

The Spiritual War for Your Soul

IT WAS A night I could not sleep. Scott was gone all night again and I had waited for him to come home or at least call me. I couldn't stand it anymore. My nerves were becoming so bad. I suffered from intense panic attacks, headaches and insomnia. I was at such a loss what to do and there was no clear direction, even from God. Divorce wasn't an option for me and God knew that. I didn't even give it much thought at this point, in case some kind of change was just around the corner, making hanging on worth it all.

Scott called in the morning and said he needed to talk when he got home. When he arrived he seemed serious, taking slow, deep breaths. He said, "You are going to get a phone call today, from a guy named Paul, Laurie's husband. I thought I should tell you first. Laurie and I have been seeing each other and Paul is her husband. He's been tapping our phone conversations."

My body began to shake and it felt as if the temperature in the room dropped twenty degrees. I couldn't stop quivering. I had this feeling when I heard about him and Marilyn, but this time it was much worse. My suspicion was right. No wonder I felt as if my very existence was being disregarded. It all began to make sense. Between feeling shock and a weird sense of relief, I went emotionally numb.

The next day came Paul's phone call. His first gruff words

were, "Your man's ass is grass!" He sounded angry, but as I spoke, he seemed to relax a little. He told me that he had recorded some of their phone conversations and their sneaky plans to escape the house and meet up somewhere. He replayed one message loud enough so that I could hear it through the phone. It made me cringe hearing their voices speak playfully to one another. Anger rose up inside as I thought of the lies and the many sleepless nights wondering where he was. *How could he betray me again after I forgave him for the Marilyn affair? Not to mention love him through my own grief?* At least I had a clear answer as to why Scott had been acting so strangely. After one year since things came out in the open about him and Marilyn, I finally had answers. At least my prayer for clarity had been answered.

I spoke a few times after that with Paul in the days ahead. I think he appreciated someone to share the pain with. His world was shattered since Laurie left him for someone else. I definitely could relate. I heard later on from Scott that Laurie said that Paul was a "safe and giving" person, and that was why Laurie married him after having previous bad relationships.

I wanted Laurie out of the picture. If I had to fight for my marriage, I couldn't do it with her in the midst. I wanted her phone number so I could call and speak to her myself. Surprisingly, Scott gave me the number to her mother's house where Laurie stayed after leaving Paul. He even asked me to record the conversation so he could hear it later! I suspected he wanted to know how Laurie would respond. He seemed positive of the fact that I would still fight for my marriage.

I first spoke with Mae, Laurie's mother. I offered her my sympathy, since she had just lost her son, Laurie's brother, in that tragic car accident. I explained who I was and that I was still fighting to save my marriage. She spoke empathetically to me about Scott and Laurie's relationship. I asked to speak with Laurie. She came to the phone and I also gave her my condolences and asked her politely to stop seeing Scott. "I want to work at my marriage and I'm not letting go." She said that it would be hard to stop, but she agreed to stop seeing him. She said that she let go of him years ago, and she would do it again. I thanked her and it was that simple, or so I thought.

Scott eventually gave me some details about their relationship including where and when things started between them. He told me that I was on to him when I was suspicious of his leaving our motel room at the Marriage Conference after he looked up her number to go get coffee.

He admitted that he had camped out many times in the car talking all night with her. His long bike rides were to meet up with her somewhere. Often, he would leave the house after I'd fallen asleep to meet with her. I was surprised about all the confessed detail I was getting from him. He talked more openly than he had in a while. In fact, at times he became very affectionate and pursued me sexually again. I was trying to understand what was going on with him. He said he had experienced this passion with Laurie that he wished he felt with me. He kissed me as if he was trying to rekindle or make that happen with me. I found this to be strange but, after so much rejection, I was strangely relishing some attention. I did figure that the passion he felt with her came as a result of his history with her, the lingering soul ties and the recent excitement they rekindled. We had experienced something like that too, when we first met and became close, but I was not the girl that broke his heart years ago, so how could I fulfill that same feeling for him? Was he comparing his feelings for the both of us to see who supplied him the most passion and connection? I had only a slight hope left in me for the future with him. He was making a curious effort, so I was willing to continue forward to at least welcome the last chance for my marriage to heal.

Scott listened to the recorded conversation I had with Laurie about staying out of my marriage. He became dissatisfied that Laurie didn't fight my demand for her to stay away from him. He later told Laurie that real love was represented by my willingness to stay with him even through all I'd been through in order to make it work. His boasting about my love for him was flattering to me, but he told me it angered her. *Was his motivation to show Laurie that if she wanted him that she would have to fight for him, just as I had, and love him with such devotion? Was it to convince her that she must love him unconditionally?* I thought to myself.

I believed he was confused about what to do and which path to choose. He spoke about what the Bible said—that leaving me for another woman was wrong and that only in the event of my death would it be acceptable to God. He even told me about a fight they had when she was tired of hearing him talk about me as if I never do anything wrong. He told me she kicked him and sped off. He even told me that it disappointed him that she gave up so easily. I thought it was over between them after that, so perhaps my love won over hers, in his mind.

One night as I was about to tuck the girls in and say our prayers, Scott wanted to join us. It had been a long time since that had happened all together as a family. We were all sitting on Jericka's bed and we all joined hands. Natasha stopped and said, "Wait! I'll be right back! God is showing me something!" She returned with a little toy treasure box and set it in front of Scott. We bowed our heads and each said a prayer before Natasha's turn. I listened and peeked out of one eye as she released my hand and pointed her five-year-old little index finger in the air. She said with authority, "I command Satan, in Jesus name, to stop trying to make Daddy choose the pile of trash instead of the treasure box with jewels in it!" I thought, *wow, was that ever God speaking through the mouth of babes!* Scott fought the tears welling up. There was another sign for him, and also for me to keep hanging on hope for our marriage and family to survive.

> *"Out of the mouths of babes and sucklings hast thou ordained strength because of thine enemies, that thou mightest still the enemy and the avenger."*
> *Psalm 8:2 KJV*

The Spiritual War for Your Soul
Key points

Understanding Spiritual Laws

If we could only see into the realm of the spirit world! There is a very real war for rights into our lives for both evil and good, all depending on our choices. God gave us the freedom to choose between two spiritual laws in which to operate. They are called: The Law of the Spirit of Life through Christ and The Law of Sin and Death. Just like natural laws, these spiritual laws don't change just because we don't like or agree with them. They should lead us to deeper wisdom by nourishing the seed of our essence.

> *"So I find this law at work: Although I want to do good, evil is there with me. For in my inner being I delight in God's law; but I see another law at work in me, waging war against the law of my mind and making me a prisoner of the law of sin at work within me."*
> *Romans 7:21-23 NIV*

The Law of Sin and Death

The law which makes us a prisoner to sin is mankind's natural bent to be proud, selfish, fearful or unyielding to the work of the Holy Spirit who God gave to guide us. We own our free will in this life and God cannot override it. The sufficient-in-ourselves egoism operates through a carnal sense of security and pleasure. It covets full control, and its own selfish rights. Just as children, at times we still want our own way, but the *strength* used through this law leads to impure outcomes that always affect the lives of others. These earthly attachments slowly darken the soul, making that person a prisoner of their own pain.

Selfishness and fear are mankind's fundamental weaknesses. Both pride and fear cause alienation from the Father. They both separate us from His love and guiding principles for mankind, causing doubt in God's ways. Doubt leads to denial, which leads to deception. Satan is the father of lies using fear and pride. God is the Father of truth using faith in His perfect love.

Faith is a spiritual muscle that requires trust; when we do, grace enables us to obey God through the trials in life. This is how we grow spiritually strong. We choose His laws by being obedient to them. God will even give us warnings through the prophetic words of others, just as He did through Natasha. "I will pour out my Spirit upon all people. Your sons and daughters will prophesy..." Acts 2:17 NLT

When battling life-changing and tempting choices, we are experiencing the pull of both laws. Choice enables these laws. The way of the flesh leads to condemning the soul; the way of the spirit leads to redeeming it. The law that is governed by the Holy Spirit will lead us toward the perfect will of God. When we yield our control to God, equipped with full spiritual armor, we sanction His plan to unfold through the Law of the Spirit of Life. Within such we live in divine protection and provision, protecting both our soul and our essence. The law governed by our own control does whatever it wants, unyielding to God's authority which actually gives power to the work of fear. Our transformation does not just happen because we are Christians but it comes as a reward for choosing to become intimately acquainted with Him. The process must be understood, respected, chosen and practiced for it to work in your life.

> *"The mind governed by the flesh is death, but the mind governed by the Spirit is life and peace. The mind governed by the flesh is hostile to God; it does not submit to God's law nor can it do so."*
> *Romans 8:6-7 NIV*

The Law of the Spirit of Life

> *"For the law of the Spirit of life in Christ Jesus has made me free from the law of sin and death."*
> *Romans 8:2 NKJV*

The Law of the Spirit of Life is governed by a Holy and loving God who seeks those who have faith in Him. When we yield to His authority, we eventually discover His blueprint is written in our hearts, and the Holy Spirit guides us on the right path. As we are being molded by His hands, we begin to resonate with His finished product: our true, pure and glorious identity. It's as if His light brings life to the seed of faith. When the Law of the Spirit of Life is at work, He is glorified through us as we overcome trials, compelling us to love others as he did. When we thank Him in the midst of the trials, it pleases Him, but also liberates us from the law of sin. No wonder Satan tries to keep people from praising and worshiping God! We become driven by love because we are His and His DNA is in our veins as he renews our minds in His truth. Abiding in the vine is abiding in the perfect Law of Life and the greatest love imaginable. Choice is powerful. To whom do you belong?

> *"For this is the love of God that we keep His commandments; and His commandments are not burdensome. For whatever is born of God overcomes the world; and this is the victory that has overcome the world—our faith."*
> 1 John 5:3-4

Prisoner by Choice

We are not our own. We were bought with a price: to glorify God in our bodies (see 1 Corinthians 6:20). God made us to be relational and wants to be one with us. He wants to be our fortress, our strength and our redeemer. We belong in relationship to God, so this is why He is jealous for you. We choose whether or not we give Him His lawful place as we follow his plan or ours. It was by choice that mankind lost this connection to begin with and by choice we can reconcile it again. He is aware of earthly idols which have a hold on our soul. He knows they won't satisfy us and we are empty without Him. He knows how to restore our true essence if only we let Him. His heart aches with love, desiring to make us whole and cleanse us from all iniquity. This is why He is jealous to be our Lord. It's not just for Him, it's for our good.

> *"You shall not bow down to them or serve them, for I the Lord your God am a jealous God, visiting t he iniquity of the fathers on the children to the third and fourth generation, of those who hate me."*
> *Exodus 20:5 ESV*

> *"Choose this day who you will serve."*
> *Joshua 24:15, paraphrased.*

Chapter 13

Takers and Nurturers

WEEKS WENT BY and it seemed that there was further communication between Scott and Laurie. This rose up the anger inside me again. I called Laurie again and reminded her to stay away from Scott. She told me this time she would not avoid seeing Scott. I wasn't as calm and polite as the last time. She mocked my use of language as not being very *Christian*! I was starting to wear thin and so was my character.

I tried to figure out what caused the turn of events. *Had Scott manipulated her to fight for him by bragging about me and my willingness to stand for my marriage?* Laurie was becoming more willing to fight for him and I was becoming less tolerant of his choices as he began to withdraw from me again. Scott criticized my faults and unkindness towards Laurie, which proved that I wasn't perfect after all. Perhaps it helped him feel more justified moving forward with her. He became distant from me again, blaming and belittling me even more. It seemed that he was moving in the direction of pursuing a relationship with Laurie. His times away from the house became more frequent.

One day I brought up my concern for him meeting our daughters' future financial needs in the event we were to divorce. I questioned the promises he made, since they'd been broken before. He became violently irritated and thrust his head into my face, giving me a nose bleed. Challenging him with such concerns became a bad idea. It was as if his choice to move forward with Laurie fueled an internal angry monster within him. I was forced to face the consequences of his choices whether I liked them or not. Perhaps this was meant to cause me fear so that I would never oppose his wayward decision with any sense of accountability for the girls.

One morning before Scott went to work and the girls were in the van ready to bring Natasha to school, his pager went off. It was Marilyn. The mere thought of her name made me see red. He said that he had been talking to her again. I didn't understand the motive and he wasn't in the mood to explain why he was talking to her. The horror of those memories arose in me and anguish was brewing about our marriage failing for good. I reacted in frustration and anger, questioning why he wanted her back in the picture now. He responded angrily to my questions. He came toward me and grabbed me by my neck, picked me up about eight inches off the floor, pinned me into the corner and pushed hard on my neck. I couldn't breathe as he started choking me. I kicked him and he threw me against the wall. I ran outside and drove away with the girls. I cried and shook uncontrollably trying very hard to keep my composure with the girls in my presence, which was very hard.

After getting Natasha to school, I asked a friend to watch Jericka for a while, as I went into the counseling office at church. Thankfully, Barb Pistagnisi was there. She comforted me and advised me to see a doctor specializing in domestic-related cases. I reluctantly went but I was not aware that they also call the police when this stuff happens. I wasn't trying to make this a bigger deal than what it was becoming.

They took pictures of my neck and the police wanted a detailed report of the incident. *What if this just causes more problems?* I was more upset about what to do than I was about what had just taken place. It was too late to reverse anything since the police were required to do their duty to follow through with their protocol in such cases. The police later came to the house to obtain his gun and bullets.

The next day he called me and I told him that I went to the police. He was furious. He said that he would probably lose his job if he has a record because he wouldn't be able to cross the border. I knew this would make him angry. *Now what have I done?* I met with the Crown Attorney to drop the charges against him. He was still ordered anger management and probation for one year.

"Precious treasure and oil are in a wise man's dwelling, but a foolish man devours it."
Proverbs 21:20 ESV

Takers and Nurturers
Key Points

The Origin of Toxicity

An underdeveloped soul manifests in different ways. Some become abusive, some remain passive, and some are codependent. The false self cannot live in conflict with their true core self and expect deep meaningful relationships. Whether you were the child who always sought to do things right or you were the child who outwardly rebelled, both can be part of a dysfunctional relationship. Even those who do things right in their own eyes may still be motivated by fear. Scott and I both were victims of incomplete childhoods in some way, lacking God-intended safety, nurture or guidance. We were each functioning in a measure of our unrecovered, unsanctified and frozen essences. We reacted our own way in our pain and confusion.

Takers may not act like bullies or abusers which makes them appear non-toxic. For example, they may have been a great friend for their mom, therefore make great listeners or a supportive friend, however, they may still be underdeveloped when it comes to being responsible, useful and attentive in other areas. Many young men who grew up without a father figure may continue to rely on a mother figure to do everything for them. They may lack initiative, courage and discipline and may not take orders well from a stronger authority figure. They may criticize how others are doing things who are at least making an effort while they are not. They may not be mindful or take serious their God-given roles as men and how such leadership would contribute to the future success of the family.

Every coping strategy used as a vice must eventually be shed like an old skin if we want God's sanctifying power to work in us. The useless outlets of denial, anger and rebellion lead to further emotional decline individually and relationally. Those who resist owning humble responsibility can only continue to function by way of their pseudo-personality or false self. A person becomes more toxic as they rely on their own system led by pride or fear. Their inner child protects the familiar immature dynamics, limiting deeper fulfilment in life and relationships

Within a healthy family system, adolescents should have learned to resist their own desires, to respect rules and show concern for other people by the time they leave home. If there was abuse or rejection prior to adolescence, they may lack those chemicals in the brain that help them control their impulses and trust authority. They will often resist selflessness or empathy for others because it leaves them powerless, just as they were as a child. As adults, they continue to protect their core by remaining isolated and/or bullying others. Instead, they may cleverly devise ways to pretend they care for others but only up to a point they feel no threat and just enough to get people off their case. The reality is that they will never escape who they really are until they recover the wounded child within.

> *"A double-minded man is unstable in all his ways."*
> *James 1:8 KJV*

Understanding the Toxic Dance

Living without surrendering the false self, people can only manage by way of deeper entanglements with the fear and/or pride driving the void inside. Some people eventually sense that something is not right. Those who live with a person in such denial pay the price in the backlash of instability, manipulation and abuse. Toxic love dynamics become routine in their relationships, replacing their damaged core essence for partial intimacy through sexual relations or other temporary fixes. Denial often leads to some form of addiction and can be difficult to identify because it's not always substance abuse. Its sinister function may operate through another person's weakness just as a substance. Like any addiction, it cycles and continues to deplete the essence of both parties in a toxic relationship.

The Roles in Abuse

Verbal and emotional abuse can be just as painful as physical abuse. Emotional torment was actually worse for me than the physical acts against me. I felt like I was beat up and left for dead as I had exposed my core essence by investing so deeply into the relationship, our children and our future. I wanted everything to work so badly, I failed to protect my own soul.

Most often, it's the nurturing personalities that fall prey to enabling those who are more bullish, self-focused or abusive. When a taker finds a nurturer, he thinks he has his soul mate since she is less likely to hold him accountable for his actions and make him bear the consequences for his unacceptable behavior. The nurturing codependent person serves as an enabling force in which the taker *plays it safe* and can easily hide their insecurities and immaturity. There is an imbalance of effort put into the relationship: more effort from the nurturer, much less from the taker. This role-play works like a dance, with both partners stuck in a pattern of self-defeat, limiting any personal and emotional growth.

A bully or taker tends to be more reactive instead of proactive. They often choose to direct personal disappointments and frustrations on others. Instead of seeing error in themselves, they may project blame on others. They are quick to point out faults in others but fail to realize what they can do to fix things in a healthy manner. Taking ownership feels risky to them. Their diversion makes them appear like the victim or the blameless one. Many people walk on eggshells around them or feel confused about what the issue was in the first place.

The bully or taker refuses to acknowledge others' feelings. They may try to disarm others or act out angrily like an immature adolescent. They remain under-developed emotionally and spiritually, caught up in his or her world of self-absorption, denial and abuse.

A taker or bully may be eighty years old yet underdeveloped and immature when it comes to intimacy in relationships. Tough love and good boundaries are required for such a person, but an enabler has difficulty establishing them. The nurturer has contributed by not providing effective ultimatums or accountability for the value of others' feelings, thoughts and input. People who are in a relationship with a taker feel trapped and hopeless. It's as if the nurturers were used as props for the takers own self-avoidance. Sometimes abusive takers exploit their non-offending partner and children as objects of their own property. Often, they eventually try to isolate the family away from others in order to remain out of view and maintain control of dysfunction.

> *"For although they knew God, they neither glorified him as God, nor gave thanks to him, but their thinking became futile and their foolish hearts were darkened."*
> *Romans 1:21 NIV*

Changing the Dance

If you are a nurturer caught in this dance, the only person that can change this dance is you. You may have to remove yourself from that position and surround yourself with safe people emotionally and physically. Learn to love yourself enough to heal your own inner child and no longer settle for this toxic relationship as it is. Understand why you contributed to this dysfunction and how your own pain drew you to this familiar personality. Love yourself enough to make it change.

At the point where abuse has crossed the line, you must use personal, emotional and/or legal boundaries for protection. Get information on the symptoms of Narcissistic Personality Disorder, Antisocial, Psychopathic and other behavior disorders, to gain clarity about what you may be dealing with.

Be warned that as you grow stronger, you may face opposition. Like me, you may be accused of being controlling. It's necessary to have effective control for your own protection and sanity. You deserve God's best and good boundaries will keep that negative force out and allow His blessings an open door into your own life. There is more on the topic of boundaries in Chapter 18.

If you choose to remain in the relationship in an effort to develop effective patterns, you must establish your boundaries and set attainable expectations without badgering the person, which would only get their defenses up more. Both you and your partner must be ready and intentional about change and should have a qualified counselor oversee the progress. This takes two people working at the restoration, not one. Be clear about your feelings and know that it's not your job to parent your partner. Know your acceptable time margins to see results. In the meantime, it's necessary for you to first discover your own identity apart from that person. They are responsible for their own growth.

"As for God, his way is perfect: The Lord's word is flawless; he shields all who take refuge in Him."
Psalm 18:30 NIV

Chapter 14

Your Transcending Reality

ONE EVENING WHEN things were calm, Scott asked me what my mom thought about him and Laurie. I told him, "Well she's not happy with you."

He responded, "I'm sick of everyone thinking that I'm always the bad guy! I'll tell you some things about your mother! She told me what went on between her and Tim when you were with him."

I calmly responded, "Really? Well, that's in the past." I acted like it was no big deal yet I was hurt to learn this. The fact that I wasn't outwardly irritated seemed to make him agitated. It was like he wanted me upset with my mom. He continued, "Your mom goes to church, raises her hands and acts so holy; there's even more about her that's not very righteous." He was showing more emotion as he spoke, "Well, there's more to that than you think."

I sensed that he wanted to tell me more. I said, "I can see that you want to tell me."

He continued somewhat unsure, "I guess we are over anyways, right?"

I said, "It seems that you are moving forward with Laurie, so I guess we are over because you're choosing that we are." He continued to talk about the time the three of us went to Las Vegas for a vacation.

I began to feel faint as I remembered that night specifically. I had been extremely tired as if my drink had been spiked as they went out without me one evening. When they came back, they were both acting strangely as if they had some little secret going on and I felt angered by it.

He went on to explain what happened when they were gone to the casino that night. They were stopped "in the act" by a parking garage attendant while they had their encounter in the car. He continued to speak of the time he went over to my mom's to help her move her television. As I listened I was quiet and just tried to breathe. He told me about their encounters at her house between them. My body began to quiver and again, the room temperature seemed to drop twenty degrees. It was that familiar state of shock that I had felt before when I'd heard of his previous affairs. *I had asked God to bring things that were hidden in to the light, didn't I?* I tried to remain calm because the more attentive I was with him, the more he would continue. These events were going on at around the same time as when he and Marilyn were involved. *Didn't he think that this would hurt me? I was so used to suppressing what I felt, perhaps he didn't think of how it affected me!*

Over the next few weeks I'd become so angry and short-fused. The added weight of further betrayal from both my mom and Scott on top of existing grief was unbearable. It was killing me that I wasn't able to be the best mom possible to my active and sometimes challenging children. It was for this reason I wanted a family life; to bring my kids up in a loving and blessed home. They didn't deserve any of this and it was getting so hard to be strong for them. Thankfully they were the very reason I had to keep focused on better days ahead.

I was so depleted of emotional and mental energy. The nighttime hours meant for sleep were filled with images in my head of my husband with other women. It was impossible to sleep even using sleeping pills. Getting through every day with all the immediate demands of school, activities, work and challenging issues was a huge task. The turmoil of not having clarity about how to deal with the situation at hand had led me to the end of myself and my dream to make this work. I felt buried under my life's efforts, which did nothing for me to this point but bring me great sorrow and grief. I mourned over my love shown to Scott, so indisputably taken for granted. My soul felt hidden underneath the wreckage of what was left over from this nightmare.

Just as I had to accept that I may never have a normal and emotionally healthy relationship with my dad, I also had to accept that I wouldn't with Scott either; at least not in this marriage to him. He was not able to connect me, God, with his inner child and true self. My lifelong quest to re-create my own family didn't end with a happily ever after. I realized there was nothing more I could do. There was little motivation to try and help him. I became more repelled by what I knew anyway. It was time to bury this dream in the ground for good.

> *"Come to me all who are weary and burdened*
> *and I will give you rest."*
> *Matthew 11:28 NIV*

Your Transcending Reality
Key Points

Emotions are Signals

We cannot heal what we cannot feel. God gave us emotions to signal when something is wrong. There is a reason why you are lacking peace. You are becoming *change-ready* as you learn to listen to your own heart again. There comes a time to let go and accept reality for what it truly is. If you disregarded your own emotions for the sake of the relationship, it's time to rediscover your lost essence and pay attention to your own growth within a new and better reality. Your changing realities are basically an accumulation of different truths, adding up to experience over time. If you continue in your familiar faulty systems, you may be resisting God's most wise, sovereign and perfect plan. God's goal is to help you see what He sees ahead of you. That's another reason to have a vision or goal, so that He can work with you to fulfill it. There are much better days ahead for you.

Let Go and Accept Change

Creating our own reality suited to our underdeveloped core is disempowering. Past wounds need to be overcome, otherwise they can keep you stuck in a fog allowing darkness to settle there. Accepting the loss of a dream or letting go of a great investment of your energy and love is difficult but never in vain. Our present realities will begin to change as we accept new ones and move beyond the familiar. Change is one of the most important elements facilitating emotional growth. It may be tough accepting that the plan faltered. It may seem like a waste that you succumbed to great suffering at the expense of another's selfishness or immaturity over many years. Learn from your experience and move forward. Christ also suffered at the hands of others. He knows how you feel and will empower you forward to a higher consciousness. Think of how this scripture applies to your situation:

"Beloved, do not think it strange concerning the fiery trial which is to try you as though some strange thing has happened to you; but rejoice to the extent that you are partakers of Christ's sufferings, that when His glory is revealed, you may also be glad with exceeding joy."
1 John 4:12-13 NKJV

That scripture is something to get excited about! Partaking of such suffering also has a side of glory to it in your future. Closing a door allows another to open. Grieve what is necessary, say goodbye to a difficult chapter and celebrate a new path of self-discovery. There are unmapped roads that you've never taken and the view is amazing when you get there! God promises to be with you through the process and seasons. There is a very valid reason for those battles even if you don't see it yet. You will be sharing the victory over these challenging times as a part of your future story of hope. You are entering a new level of freedom from the prison of emotional captivity. Your story and journey has yet to be discovered.

"The Spirit of the Lord God is upon me, because the Lord has anointed me to bring good news to the poor: he has sent me to bind up the brokenhearted, to proclaim liberty to the captives: and the opening of the prison to those who are bound."
Isaiah 61:1 ESV

The Truth Within Your Essence

People will judge what they do not understand. Your reality is different from others because of your own unique experiences. All humans have their own *illusions* of truth. In principle, everyone's reality is at a present stage of their overall life experience. Many remain in their maladaptive truth until they are faced with trauma. I see people's reality change suddenly as they re-evaluate what's important on a larger and eternal scale. Most people who had near death experiences are greatly affected. In my opinion, people who have survived terrible suffering or tragedy and have overcome them with upright character and strength have a more accurate sense of truth. Scripture states that even Jesus learned obedience from what He suffered. (See Hebrews 5:8) If you desire to grow, you must be willing to adjust your beliefs, which may also mean changing some negative influences around you. Move toward a higher truth such as the one Jesus operated in. He is our model of influence, victory and love.

Be prepared to let go of former soul ties with a person whose reality is not transcending with yours. Be willing to admit that you had accepted an illusion for a time. As you pursue your own calling in life, people may not understand or support your growth. There comes a time when you must take it up with God alone, through an intimate exchange with the One who *is* transcendent reality. Only He can know the depth of your emotions. He can lead you into all truth and to higher ground with a better view. He waits for you to take His hand and let Him show you the way.

"…that is the Spirit of truth, whom the world cannot receive, because it does not see Him or know Him, but you know Him because He abides with you and will be in you. I will not leave you as orphans; I will come to you."
John 14:17-18 NASB

Chapter 15

Lover of My Soul

SCOTT WAS OUT somewhere. The girls were sound asleep. It was 1:30 a.m. I was battling anger against Scott for resisting the love I had given him and the sacrifices I had made. I needed to be real with God and let Him know I was getting angry at Him also. I felt that He had forsaken me. He let me down, even throughout all of the surrendering I had done and immense grief I felt, even since my childhood. I sat down on the floor in front of the window sill of the large bay window facing the front yard. If only I could break down and cry. I needed an emotional release from all the tension I've been holding inside for months. *God I can't go on like this without your help!* After a while, still with a heavy heart, I turned on the song that got me through many of the down times, "The Power of Your Love," by Hillsongs.

Lord I come to you
Let my heart be changed, renewed
Flowing from the grace
That I found in You
And Lord I've come to know
The weaknesses I see in me
Will be stripped away
By the power of Your love

Hold me close
Let your love surround me
Bring me near
Draw me to Your side
And as I wait
I'll rise up like the eagle
And I will soar with You
Your Spirit leads me on
In the power of Your love

Lord unveil my eyes
Let me see You face to face
The knowledge of Your love
As You live in me
Lord renew my mind
As Your will unfolds in my life
In living every day
By the power of Your love

The words ministered profoundly as I envisioned Jesus holding me close, comforting me. The song drew out intense emotions from deep in my soul. I opened my heart to Him again and brought every pain, question, concern and angry feeling out in the open to Him. From the hidden corners of my heart came memories of my childhood leaving my soul feeling raw. I sobbed as if I was pulling pain out of my gut. I knew my prayers and cries reached His heart. It was as if He cried with me as He held me close to His chest. When the pain released, I became calm and just listened to what He might say.

I wanted answers to so many questions which crept in as doubts were challenging my faith: *Where do I go from here? Does this mean it is over?* I thought back to when I trusted in God's direction before marrying Scott. *What does the bouquet landing at my feet mean now? I thought You gave me that promise for my family? God...you know I would continue to try to save this marriage, but if only I knew what you wanted me to do! None of this makes sense to me right now! I relied on You then for answers and I still rely on You giving me an answer now! Please don't leave me hanging raw like this!*

> *"The wind blows where it wishes, and you hear the sound of it, but cannot tell where it comes from and where it goes. So is everyone who is born of the spirit."*
> *John 3:8 NKJV*

It was dark outside and the trees swayed as the wind blew stronger, as if a storm was approaching. *There it is again, another déjà vu moment: Looking out the window, reminiscing over the painful childhood despair of my collapsing family, questioning the future. God you know I never wanted my girls to experience a family out of control. The very thing I wanted for my girls was what my childhood lacked; a safe haven where daddy and mommy both watch over and love their children. My girls need that balance and I don't know how to do both roles. I want to believe that you care about us all. I know you saw me back then, just as You do now.*

It was like He was bringing me back to that early memory on purpose. I didn't want to carry that childhood burden anymore; I was willing to rid its anguish from my heart. It was not my burden to carry as a child, though my mind believed that, somehow, it still was.

After crying over the memories, I soon began to feel a peaceful release as I sat and gazed at the trees fiercely blowing. I imagined His love and comfort consoling and reassuring my searching heart. The biggest question that remained was about the bouquet that landed at my feet. It still represented God's promise to me: *I know you don't break your promises God; if I let go of this marriage now, then what did the significance of the bouquet landing at my feet mean? I relied on that with childlike faith, knowing that it was a sign from you to marry Scott, after the previous bouquet caused me injury and pain. I depended on you to show me, since I had no other healthy direction in my life. You were the only Father who I could turn to and trust with my heart. This part is still not clear!*

In this sweet communion with Him, I knew deep inside that I would somehow get an answer. His loving-kindness wouldn't just leave me hanging like this. The only thing that came to mind were the same words I shared at my wedding speech: *By the wind of my Spirit I will bring him to you,* were the words that kept coming to me, which were also the words I thought confirmed how He brought Scott into my life. The wind mysteriously picked up even stronger as if He confirmed what I had just thought. Okay, I thought, perhaps the wind would blow me some kind of answer to clarify its meaning as I waited. *Maybe a paper would blow with a message on it or some type of sign?* Nothing was blowing toward me. But I thought of the wind and its mysterious ways—that only God knows what it carries and when it changes, just as only God knows our future.

Then out of the dark windy night, a basketball came rolling along the curb, hugging it, as it rounded the corner and continued down my street. I watched it roll, knowing that the wind was pushing it along the curb. God was again using the wind to show me something; but a basketball? It continued to roll along the curb and the wind suddenly died down to such stillness and so did the ball. In fact it stopped dead center in front of me. I waited and thought, *well, maybe the message is on the ball.* I walked outside as the wind was still calm. I picked up the basketball, brought it inside and looked it over. There was the number *23* and the word *Wilson* on it. Hmm, I thought. *Was this to confirm that, yes, God said that He would send my husband to me? But then, what does it mean, now that things have come to this point in my marriage?* It still wasn't clear, but I did feel better after such a refreshing time with God. His former promise of the wind of His spirit bringing my husband to me remained His word of promise for me. I still chose to accept that sign was significant, whatever it meant at that point. He would show me more about this. Hope began to grow as I knew in my heart that He had not forsaken His promises. I believed He cared enough to show me this much. *God, please give this more clarity soon*, I prayed.

> *"For you do not delight in sacrifice, otherwise I would give it;*
> *You are not pleased with burnt offering. The sacrifices of God*
> *are a broken spirit: A broken and a contrite heart,*
> *O God, You will not despise."*
> *Psalm 51:16-17 NASB*

It was summer and I was so thankful we had a pool. I had class parties for the girls; their friends would come over and it kept them making happy memories. I had invited Chantelle and her then four kids and Veronica and her then three kids. It was ironic that we were all going through the same thing at the same time with our marriages. We had all attended a support group at our church called "Just me and the Kids." There was a children's portion of the program where the kids could understand and grow from the challenges as children of broken homes. We needed each other's support and friendship at that time and we were like family, making it a daily routine to eat together and talk about our days.

As the children played in the water, I spoke to my two friends about my recent experience of emotionally unloading to God a few nights ago. I explained to them the background of what the two bouquets represented to me and that I knew God was guiding me through these events; the first bouquet that hit me in the face which caused me pain and embarrassment was supposed to represent me trying to make a marriage happen in my timing. The next bouquet which was miraculously timed to hit the ceiling fan, sending it to my feet, represented how Scott came in my life. Then I explained to them that the sudden appearance of the Wilson basketball meant that God's promise still holds true. Just as mysterious as the wind, I couldn't interpret the meaning of His promise relating to my broken marriage.

Chantelle responded right away and said: "Don't you see it, Chris? The first bouquet, that caused you pain, shame and despair could only represent your marriage with Scott and what it caused you! So the second bouquet represents the next marriage that God will orchestrate and how He will be involved miraculously! God's faithful promise to you still remains!"

I thought about what she said and replied, "Wow, Chantelle you're right, I never looked at it that way!"

She added, "I'd be keeping that ball around until God shows you what it means." She was right. God's promise still holds true; that He would send my *next* husband to me, fulfilling His promise to me after all. The Wilson ball gave me a hint for what lay ahead in the future with the next marriage.

The interpretation of the promise gave me the release to

move forward and close this chapter of my life. God showed me that was exactly the paradox of the first bouquet. I had been so bent on not divorcing Scott; I could not see what this marriage was. It was so painfully broken I could no longer do anything to fix it. God knew I would need an interpretation because I was so bent on hanging on to it. Sometimes, that's what true friends are for. They speak into your life, drawing us to the truth of the Father's love. I contacted a lawyer to draw up a divorce.

The hard realities about the marriage ending were things like the drawings on the fridge that Natasha and Jericka had done. Lately, they were about family with four people, all holding hands, with hearts, and the words *love* and *God* written all around the family unit. My heart was grieved, remembering my own childhood fears. On the other hand, I was relieved, knowing it was time to move forward. I'd done all I could do to save my marriage. I knew I needed only to please God from now on. I chose to believe that He had better days ahead for my daughters and me.

I would accept my new identity as a divorcee. It was harder to accept that I would no longer be the daughter-in-law, the sister-in-law or the aunt to members of his family. Even though it was hard, I prepared myself for further grief and rejection. My failed marriage was not the end of my story; it's only part of my story.

Lover of My Soul
Key Points

"The greatest moments in life are the miraculous moments when divine omnipotence and human inability intersect, when we bring impossible situations to God and invite Him to intervene."
Lance Wallnau

Quantum Attraction

Miracles, divine connections and coincidences challenge our logic. I believe they are meant to get us thinking about the mysterious side of God and to admit we don't have all the answers. Albert Einstein said, "Imagination is more important than knowledge." We are all wise in our own eyes because nothing is true to us until we relate to it. Having childlike imagination is better than our own human intellect because being wise in our own eyes limits us. Jesus said; "Truly I tell you, anyone who will not receive the kingdom of God like a little child will never enter it" (Mark 10:15 NIV). When we are *change ready* and we earnestly pray to God for answers, it moves His heart to action.

"Faith is the substance of things hoped for the
evidence of things not seen."
Hebrews 11:1 KJV

Modern physics research has embraced metaphysical concepts. There is increasing focus on the Natural Laws of the Universe which help to confirm that there are vibrational attractions through our words and actions, both positive and negative. Even the advances of science accept that quantum mechanics exceed the laws of physics. Miracles need an explanation to the human logic. Arriving at these facts means that researchers have reached their intellectual fork in the road. More people will believe that God Himself wants to interact with mankind. Jesus did this years ago and instructed us to follow His example. This is no groundbreaking idea like many people think it is. His example taught us to operate in these spiritual and natural laws as He was humanity and deity. As believers we have an even higher spiritual right to these divine laws, when we abide in the fullness of His presence in our lives.

Quantum mechanics and various paths to enlightenment closely parallel Jesus's teachings. They are catching up with the scriptures' authors who have already defined these truths. There is one big difference; the universe is not a person. Why do people ask of something that is not personable? I believe that Satan seeks to take our focus off the very person who already gave us instructions in the Bible. No wonder he has worked so hard to remove the Christian Bible; it's richly loaded with powerful truth for every type of misery to mankind! The bible signifies the truth in the person of Jesus Christ, as it states in John 1:14 that; "the word became flesh and dwelt among us." He was tempted in every way yet did not sin. Hebrews 4:15.

Physics and the Bible agree on so many levels. Many people are so close to the truth yet lack of the personal connection with the God who rules the universe. When a person's desperate faith-filled heart converges with a loving God, He may order His own creation as He chooses to bring about a message, an event or miracle. I have no doubt that in those moments for me, I was connecting to my God, to whom I know I belong. His comforting, understanding and all-knowing heart breathed hope to me, compassionately sending His answer to my desperate questioning soul.

"Through whom we have also obtained access by faith into this grace in which we now stand, and we boast in the hope of the glory of God."
Romans 5:2 ESV

Love Takes Two

God wants an intimate connection with us. He knocks and waits for us to open our hearts doors because He wants that deep relationship with us. Because He gives us free will, He will not barge down the door. When we open the door, invite Him in, seek His ways, bond with and follow Him, His faithful blessings are rewards, just as a the perfect parent gives his children. Storms in life are meant to teach us that defiance brings separation but unconditional love welcomes us home, like the perfect parent would, just as in the Prodigal Son passage in the bible. Coming home to be loved and forgiven by the one who knows best, makes us feel confident that we belong to Him. He rejoices in our discoveries about Him. There is no human being that can offer this intimate connection with our soul and spirit. Millions of people on earth can attest to this.

"Trust in the Lord with all your heart, and lean not on your own understanding, in all your ways acknowledge Him and He shall direct you paths."
Proverbs 3:5 NKJV

No matter how old we are, we are still in the process of spiritual maturity. As long as there is still life to live, we simply pick up where we left off and revive our lost essence. Every storm brings a lesson. In the midst of it, ask Him what to do. Storms in life are meant to cause us to question if we are in faith or in fear. They remind us of our need to have total dependence on His leading and have peace in the midst of the storm.

It doesn't matter how long it's been or how impossible things look, all the forces of darkness can't stop what God will do when our heart is right with Him. Never think it's too late! He is still waiting.

> *"For precept must be upon precept, precept upon precept, line upon line, line upon line, here a little, there a little."*
> *Isaiah 28:10 NKJV*

Prayer: Jesus, You are my closest companion and friend. You understand everything I feel and will guide me from this point forward. You are always accessible. Father, you are the perfect parent whose arms are open, welcoming me home. You know me better than anyone. I'm an adult child still learning. You are the only One who knows if I'm on the right path and where I missed the mark. Help me to hear from you. I ask You to move in my circumstances so I can be guided to do Your will in my life.

> *"For my thoughts are not your thoughts, neither are your ways my ways, declares the Lord. As the heavens are higher than the earth, so are my ways higher than your ways and my thoughts than your thoughts."*
> *Isaiah 55:8-9 NIV*

Chapter 16

Grace to Choose Right

I MADE IT through Mother's Day and would not let anger or injustice win over my life and relationships. I gave my mom a huge arrangement of flowers to honor her as my mom. For the first week it was harder to hide the anger inside about what I knew, but I still chose to. I was disappointed but I surely didn't want to hate her. She was my mom and I knew that she had a horrible childhood and she had lost her way on the straight and narrow path. I understood how things can easily happen when we are vulnerable. I yielded my feelings and words and determined in my heart to forgive her and wait before I said anything to her about it.

The following week, I cried all my disappointment out to my Heavenly Daddy and felt His peace come over me afterward. I felt His grace moving me to talk to my mom about what Scott told me. I knew that my anger had diminished and I was prompted to show her love and forgiveness. That Sunday, she invited the girls and me over to her house for brunch. As we did the dishes together, my heart began to race as I rehearsed in my mind how to begin to talk to her. Confrontation was sometimes difficult for me. I put a video in for the girls, so there would be less chance of interruption. I asked her to come into her bedroom so we could talk. I took her hand and I said, "I want you to know that I know about you and Scott and all that happened. I forgive you and I want you to forgive yourself." We hugged and it felt so good to speak those words.

She was quiet at first, probably unsure just what to say but eventually she said, "I don't know how I could have done this to my own daughter."

My mom had been abused sexually and emotionally by her dad as a child. She had very little healing from her past, which helped me understand how something like this could have happened. I was just thankful I learned about Marilyn first, because by then, after learning about Scott and my mom, I was starting to feel the pain of it all less. I was beginning to see the picture more clearly. I was also growing stronger emotionally.

Scott questioned why I would forgive my mom, yet I wouldn't forgive Marilyn. My response was, "I can forgive Marilyn, but I still don't trust her." I didn't know if she would somehow take more away from my life, or confuse my children. *Would she spoil them and say bad things to them about me?* I just wasn't ready. The girls even persisted to allow her to come.

I was confused as to why he wanted her around again since the hatred he displayed towards her a while back. He had even told Natasha and Jericka that she did something bad earlier.

Months passed and Laurie and Scott got married. From that point on, their relationship with Marilyn began to worsen and they stopped having any contact with her. Whatever was going on seemed to bring about those vicious angry emotions toward Marilyn again.

A few months later I received a phone call from Marilyn. She asked if she could speak to the girls, and that she had some gifts she'd like to send them. I was reluctant because of the past and told her that I wasn't sure I could trust her. She talked about the counseling she had received and the church she was attending. She had learned a lot about the dynamics of reunions with mothers and sons. She explained some of the details of the inappropriate encounters with Scott.

I allowed her to send the girls some gifts, and eventually allowed her to come and visit. I found it easier to forgive her, now that she had made some significant steps and took responsibility for her part in the relationship of the past. It became liberating for me to allow forgiveness to flow to her. I didn't want to stay angry and in my heart it was the right thing to do to show forgivness. She continued to talk a lot about Scott and she hoped things would be normal between them someday. He had totally cut her off and Marilyn spoke of how hurt she was and how cruel he'd been to her. I no longer felt that she was a threat to me or my daughters. She was a big help in fact, offering to stay with my daughters while I went to work instead of hiring a babysitter. I went out with friends for some social time, while she spent time with her grandchildren.

Scott learned that Marilyn was coming over more frequently and staying with us. One of her visits ended in a quite upsetting way. As Marilyn began loading her belongings into her car to drive back to Ottawa, she entered the front door crying. I looked at her and she stood there with a large dead fish partially wrapped in newspaper obituaries. She sobbed as she tried to say Scott's name. After I got her calmed down, she said, *Scott told me if I tried to contact you and the girls, that I was dead meat. That is what this means!!... I know it!*

The Grace to Choose Right
Key Points

*"Create in me a clean heart, O God, and renew a
right spirit within me."*
Psalm 51:10 ESV

Choosing Love Builds Character

Developing our character is an option in life which involves intentionally choosing our emotions. Since our emotions are linked to our beliefs, when our beliefs change, aligning our emotions is easier. By eliminating what is false, we accept higher truth. When our union with God is strengthened, emotional triggers are not as fueled with an urge to defend ourselves. Choosing a higher truth sets us free to be authentic, regardless of how others see us. Having love-grounded and steadfast beliefs allows His grace to help us do what's right. It does not mean we are weak. It actually is meekness, which is strength under control. An angry heart chokes the seed of faith. Forgiving allows His seed to grow. When you nourish it with scriptures, your heart becomes better soil. In time, you will see a higher purpose unfold. Pruning the old ineffective ways allows for new growth, when it's nourished by His love.

> *"God is working in you, giving you the desire to obey him and the power to do what pleases him."*
> *Philippians 2:13 NLT*

Be a Master—not a Slave—of Emotions

Ruminating over injustices attracts more darkness, making us slaves to our emotions, not a master over them. There are times we need to give when it hurts, deny our fleshly appetites until it hurts and even praise God when it hurts. It's never in vain, though our flesh may argue, especially when it's unpopular. Genuine sacrifice and surrender expands us to grow in character. Internal peace confirms this fact. It feels right. Choosing your thoughts is emotional intelligence in action. Mastering our emotions builds healthy pathways in our brains. Eventually, like any other habit, doing the right thing becomes easier since we are less consumed with feelings that don't have a positive outcome. With a vision for the future, and God's promises in your heart, we stay focused on what's ahead instead of staying stuck where we are.

> *"No weapon that is formed against me shall prosper, and every tongue that shall rise against thee in judgment thou shalt condemn. This is the heritage of the servants of the Lord, and their righteousness is of me saith the Lord."*
> *Isaiah 54:17 KJV*

Gratitude Energy

Complaining robs us of the blessed future God has in store. Being thankful for God's sovereignty allows our focus to be on His faithfulness, not our trials.

Consider Christ's life and how He mastered His emotions, trusting His Father until death. He never complained, which allowed God's will to be done. He is known to have had the highest vibrations of light and energy, not consumed with self-pity or pride. He was fully engaging His true essence of love, which translated into the power to work miracles. He was so tightly connected to His Heavenly Father and the goal set before Him. This was faith and obedience in action.

Satan hates when we choose to walk out God's plan for us, because it confounds his plan. Dark accusations may come as a result of choosing to do right. Regardless of where those accusations lead, or the lies that may be told, don't fall prey to feeling a need to vindicate yourself. Focus on your future and don't worry about your reputation. That is God's job and He's the one who judges if you're hitting the mark toward your purpose and calling. God protects His plan for your life.

Guard your heart from an impure motive. Only light puts out darkness, not the other way around. Self-righteousness for human gain is still darkness and equal to doing wrong. Doing right for the right reason is true light; benefiting the relationship with both God and others.

"For the Lord will vindicate His people and have
compassion on His servants."
Psalm135:14 ESV

Jesus Vibrations

There is victory over all pain and sin upon us, even when it appears that the perpetrator is getting the last word. God always has the final say and is eternally just. Look at the resurrection of Christ as proof of His justice! He eventually attained victory over death itself because of the life of love He willingly displayed.

Because He did, we too can be compensated for every measure of suffering and injustice in this life. What a power to tap into! No other person on earth has ever reached such high vibrational frequencies as Jesus. He was interconnected in oneness with His Father, the God of the Universe. In the same way with the same grace, we have the ability to be overcomers of the darkness in this life. When we suffer from what others have done to us, we can trust that choosing right will never be in vain. He promised to turn it all around for good through you and for His glory. Trusting in God's truth and justice is a sign of spiritual maturity and emotional intelligence. Thank Him in advance for His love and faithfulness.

"For I am persuaded, that neither death, nor life, nor angels or principalities, nor powers, nor things present, nor t hings to come, nor height, nor depth, nor any other creature, shall be able to separate us from the love of God, which is in Christ Jesus our Lord."

Romans 8:38-39 KJV

Chapter 17

Only One Life

THROUGHOUT THE YEARS, my mom continued to help three of her brothers at different times, by allowing them to live in the house. She carried a burden on her heart for her younger siblings since she was like a mom to them when they were children. This was a familiar role that was dragging her back into old habits. Over the last few years, her standards had been compromised by the reminiscent smells of marijuana, tastes of alcohol and people from the past entering the home.

A few years previous, my mom had major surgery for an aortic aneurism. She did quit smoking for about one year, but ignoring the doctor's warning, she began smoking again after my Uncle Jim's suicide.

One day she told me some horrible news. She had a large lymph node removed from her collar bone area. The biopsy report revealed she had stage three cancer. Doctors ran a series of tests, but were unclear on the primary source, since nothing showed up in her chest x-ray even though they suspected lung cancer. She would be given a random treatment of chemotherapy to begin fighting it.

Yvette and I would take turns to get her groceries and do household chores. On my shifts I juiced vitamin-rich and cancer-fighting foods. We incorporated a holistic diet to cleanse her body, fight the cancer cells and strengthen her immune system.

We weren't happy with the guessing treatment from the Windsor doctors and wanted the best medical technology possible. We drove to London University Hospital and they tried a new approach to treatment. It seemed she made progress for a month or so but she began to suffer terrible pain in her leg, probably from something developing in her lower back near her spine. Doctors did radiation on the area but this only caused greater pain. Her white blood cells counts were too low to handle any more chemotherapy. Her times at the hospital became longer and eventually she was moved to the Oncology floor, only for pain control. It was a horrible time, feeling helpless as we watched her decline.

My mom wanted to see my dad. He was married to his third wife at the time. She worked for a doctor and she was kind enough to support him visiting my mom. We began shifts to be with her, between Yvette, my dad and I. It was nice to see my dad show such concern for her. He made a point to be there for us in every way he could. He truly cared and I loved to see that side of him.

The battle was ten months long thus far. There was nothing more the doctors could do. Her mental condition worsened and distressing dementia started its horrible effects. We saw her decline in a way that was horrifying for her but also tormenting emotionally to all of us seeing her.

Life during this time was so hectic from non-stop activity with school and extracurriculars, leaving little time to process everything emotionally. My sister's children were ages nine, six and three. My daughters were seven and four. They all loved their grandma. It was important to walk them through this difficult time as well.

I was consumed with so many stressors; at times it was hard to think straight. The last few years were like a horrible nightmare. Everything seemed to be happening all at once, and so soon after things were ending with Scott. *Why?* I thought. *Could it be that my mom didn't want to live with the truth out about what had happened between them? I know I had truly forgiven her and frequently told her to forgive herself. God knew the answers and I'm sure there is a merciful one when it came to her eternity.*

It was my birthday and nothing about it so far was happy. I knew my mom was dying. Seeing her decline every day at the hospital made me feel weary and emotionally exhausted. While visiting her, I took a break and went for a walk and prayed to God, *Heavenly Father, being that it's my birthday, could you show me something from your heart that is from you and you alone? I ask you as a daughter would ask her daddy. I know that you know this hurt in my heart right now.* I knew He heard me and that something special would come from Him.

I returned to Mom's room to find Pastor Rick at my mom's side. She spoke to me saying, "I told him everything, Chris, about, well, you know..."

I said, "I'm glad you could talk to him. Do you feel better now?"

She said, "Yes, but I'm very tired, I probably should sleep. Thank you Father, I mean, Pastor for coming!" We all chuckled at her words.

Pastor Rick said, "What she said is ironic, because I was recently given a new title as the Father of the Open Bible Faith Fellowship!"

Pastor Rick and I left and walked to the atrium and sat down and I said to him, "I am so glad she was able to talk to you."

He said, "Your mom was concerned that it was wrong that your dad was coming to see her and kiss her, even though he's married.

I replied, "Oh, is that what she meant? I thought she told you about something else." I hesitated, but then I thought I could expound more openly, since I knew that what I would say was in good hands. I tried to stop the tears as I told him the history between my mom and Scott.

He was so compassionate and hugged me like a father would, which made me cry even more. He said, "I am so very proud of you!" His words were as if I was hearing them from my heavenly Father, as God knew my struggle inside as if somehow I had something to do with her decline.

"I sense no guile in you whatsoever about everything that happened between them," he said. It was the very thing I needed to hear as if those words came from my Heavenly Father. God knew my thoughts, and I believe He wanted me to know that He was pleased with me.

As Pastor Rick and I left the atrium and walked down the hospital hall to the elevator, I realized that what had just happened was an answer to my earlier prayer. I told Pastor Rick that it was my birthday and I had specifically asked God to do something for my birthday that could only be from God as my Father. God had sent my very busy pastor today to tell me, just as a Father would, that he was proud of me. Only God knew that was needed for my desperate heart. As a child I assumed bad things that happened were somehow my fault. God's fatherly concern for those damaging lies was shown to me that day through my pastor.

My mom's suffering ended peacefully on April 5th, with my Dad, Yvette and me by her side. She was fifty-eight years old. I could only rejoice with her as she entered into the loving arms of her Savoir, Jesus, and the comfort of her Heavenly Father.

"Dear friends, let us love one another, for love comes from God. Everyone who loves has been born of God and knows God. Whoever does not love does not know God because God is love. This is how God showed His love among us; He sent His one and only Son into the world, that we might live through Him."
1 John 4:7-9 NIV

Only One Life
Key Points

The Need to Grieve

We must never deny the need to grieve since it must run its course for necessary healing. Grieving a loss means saying goodbye to a person, a dream or a goal. It's the closing of a chapter in life. Overcoming grief and loss happens in stages. Whether it's the loss of a loved one, betrayal or a failed relationship, grieving is necessary.

Hope and acceptance are part of the latter phases and are necessary for emotional and spiritual growth. Healing times vary for everyone. Closure can be very difficult and may take years for some. For me, I had accepted the loss of my mom incrementally as I watched her decline. I was willing to move forward past so much sadness in my life. I was confident that one day I would see her again in heaven.

"Death has been swallowed up in victory."
1 Corinthians 15:54.

Confidence for Eternity

The reality of death and the hereafter can be tormenting or relieving depending on one's beliefs. In the past, I feared death terribly but when we are in God's trustworthy hands we need not fear death. There is proof that it is not the final outcome. It simply means we are transferred from this earthly realm to the spiritual. Only the shell is left behind. When our soul has been touched by His love and continues to grow, less fear about death remains.

"Because your steadfast love is better than life,
my lips will praise you."
Psalm 63:3 ESV

There is no firmer foundation than one built on the Rock of Jesus Christ. He was the human expression of God's love and power over every evil in this life, promising eternal victory. God will not waste any hardship without having some purpose behind it. Whether you realize it or not, you would be happiest and most fulfilled in His will for your life, operating in the inner strength He has provided. Why would you not want a relationship that supplies you with the very peace, security and power your heart longs for?

He restores my soul; He leads me in paths of r
ighteousness for his name's sake."
Psalms 23:3 ESV

Stewards of our Lives

"He has made everything beautiful in its time. He has also set eternity in the human heart; yet no one can fathom what God has done from beginning to end."
Ecclesiastes 3:11 NIV

We will all likely have a final day here on earth. The stewardship of our time on earth will reveal the wisdom we've gained here. We are all given a choice to accept the security of an eternity with God and the saints who trusted in the shed blood and empty grave of Jesus Christ. Victory over sin and death is our blessed hope. But heaven doesn't start in heaven. It starts when we allow His incorruptible nature inside our core essence, our heart. That's when the work of grace begins within us and continues with each obedient moment of surrender. Your true essence unfolds as you allow Him to shepherd your soul.

"So when this corruptible has put on incorruption, and this mortal has put on immortality, then shall be brought to pass the saying that is written: 'Death has been swallowed up in victory.'"
1 Corinthians 15:54 NKJV

I believe that our time here on earth is our opportunity to grow spiritually, preparing our true essence for pure and sinless heaven, as we are guided by His word and Spirit. If Heaven is about holiness, selflessness and pure love, then only that which is sanctified and surrendered to His redemptive love is worthy of His presence. No flesh will be glorified as stated in 1 Corinthians 1:29 KJV; "that no flesh may glory in His presence." We can achieve redemption through obedience and grace, not of mere flesh. I believe that obedient measure of grace defines who we are in eternity. Why not live that essence out here on earth if it's available to you?

"Teach us to number our days that we may gain a heart of wisdom."
Psalm 90:12 NIV

Have you used your days here with eternity in mind, conscious of life's brevity? Have you gone through the motions of righteous living without experiencing intimate experience with Jesus? Keep in mind that you have a purpose here on earth and it is to glorify God, not ourselves. In the end, our life won't be all about us, but about what His grace has done in us. We have from childhood to old age to influence those around us, giving those we touch access to His truth as we become willing vessels of His love.

It is my belief that at times in His infinite mercy God allows an early end of life, even in tragedy. It seldom makes earthly sense but in the scope of God's omnipotent wisdom, there is a reason for it. One day He will prove His majestic justice and mercy to those who trust in His unfailing love. The proof of this fact is the knowledge that the tragic early death of His son was not in vain. Death had no power over Him.

"Precious in the sight of the Lord is the death of His saints."
Psalm 116:15 KJV

"Knowing that Christ being raised from the dead dieth no more; death hath no more dominion over Him."
Romans 6:9 KJV

Final Justice

"In Him we have redemption through His blood, the forgiveness of our trespasses, according to the riches of His grace."
Ephesians 1:6 NRSV

This world system is not always fair and just. People escape justice every day. Victims of terrible crimes may never feel compensated for their suffering through our earthly justice system. Family lives may have been unfair and people play favorites on the job. It's easy to slip into hopelessness when injustice seems to win. We can find hope and justice when we look to God as a fair, merciful and just judge. God knows why people hurt and why they are emotionally stuck. He knows the human injustice and the hardships resulting from ignorant and selfish people. For those reasons especially, He wants to prove his love for us, regardless of our imperfections. Owning our imperfections should compel us to change. He remains faithful to us, but will you let Him show that He is?

God is trustworthy. Jesus trusted His Father through a grueling and unjust death with dying grace. The evidence of God's faithfulness and justice led to Jesus's glorious resurrection. That was the proof that love destroyed death itself. Every drop of blood He shed for us was not in vain. The grace sowed through suffering will be reaped with glory for those who would receive His redeeming power. This same grace helps us press on toward the mark of the high calling of Christ (See Philippians 3:14). His struggles were not in vain, nor will your trials be when they are for His sake. Jesus is our model of God's faithfulness and justice.

God's government is trustworthy. When we resist God's control, refusing His direction and laws without trusting Him, we become our own government, trying to control our destiny. When people reject God's control, they also are rejecting His protection, His plan and His blessings. It's like pulling the shore to the boat instead of pulling the boat to the shore. There are so many viewpoints in today's world operating this way. Thank God that this world system is not the final outcome from all we go through! What will your life message be?

"He that dwelleth in the secret place of the most high shall abide under the shadow of the Almighty."

Psalm 91:1 KJV

Chapter 18

Actualizing Your New Truth

THE DAYS AHEAD were very busy since we had my mom's house to empty and sell. One day Yvette had stopped at my mom's house. She called me from there and explained to me that she and her husband had an argument, so she went to the house, missing our mom's presence for support. As she talked I heard a ringing noise. While we talked, the other phone was ringing! That was strange, we thought.

Another day I was at my mom's house and the phone rang. I answered it and I heard nothing but static. I just hung up and in a few more minutes it happened again. I decided that something must be wrong with that phone, so I unplugged it from the outlet and from the phone line. *There, now it wouldn't ring any more*, I thought. A few minutes later, the same phone which I unplugged, again, began to ring. *That was strange. How could that be?*

When I got home that evening, my bathroom clock began ticking backwards and from then on for weeks it continued exactly on time, but only going back in time. I connected these two events as a message of meaning. I believed from these strange occurrences that God was impressing on my heart that if my mom could turn back time and be free from the darkness she had in life, there would be so much she would have said to us! In my heart I believed that my mom's heart was kind and at her core, her love for us was greater than her wounded soul was able to show us. I understood her terrible struggles and so did our merciful God. I believe that her prayers for us over the years were still heard on the days she was without answers for us.

My mom's estate and affairs were nearly complete and we sold the house and car. There was money left over after funeral expenses from the sale of the house. My sister was going through a hostile divorce and now had three children to care for on a tighter budget, so a little extra help during her difficult time was welcome. For me, having a little extra money meant I could take a much-needed vacation and put some aside to help with my girls' education. I had a new roof and some new windows and repairs done on our house. I even gave Scott some money against my lawyer's advice. I loaned money to friends in need. I felt a certain sense of value in doing so.

About two years after Mom's passing, I opened myself up to date. I met Tom, who also had been divorced and had two kids of his own. At first I wasn't attracted to him, but he was so nice and fun, which made me attracted to him. He treated me so differently from Scott, it was refreshing. He was great with kids, and my girls liked him.

He enlightened me to some of the processes with child support, and advised that I get an update on Scott's income since for four years he had been making more money and the support payments were supposed to be adjusted accordingly.

Tom had helped me to begin implementing those changes and I believe Scott saw this as a personal attack. I was beginning to take control of things that were my duty and right as a custodial parent. I had to face the fear I had of him, which normally came over me at such times. I had to do the right things for the girls and me. An attorney's involvement in the process made settlement issues even more intense. I would rather not have involved attorneys but I had no choice because Scott would not communicate without using intimidating and painful responses.

I began to see another side of Scott, similar to what I saw displayed toward Marilyn, when he turned against her using cruel words. Even though Scott and I moved on in our separate lives, I knew it angered him that I started to stand up to him more, use firmer boundaries and make choices he didn't like. I was speaking for myself and the girls needs now. He started to turn on me as if I were the most hated and disgusting person on earth. His intense words were so evil and heart-wrenching. He criticized my voice and bodily features, and swore viciously at me with every opportunity. He called Tom and I names, he told lies to his family about me. He left vile messages on the phone with hateful words.

My panic attacks became worse, especially while hearing his voice messages or opening mail containing awful comments oozing with hate. I was baffled by his lack of conscience for these spiteful words and it scared me. *After all of the forgiveness and kindness that I extended to him after the infidelity, how could he be this way?* This brought on feelings of rejection and hurt inside me as I thought of how he negated the worth of my sacrifices to him. *How could any human do this to someone without any compassion or remorse for the pain he's inflicted?* I questioned God many times, *why won't you make him stop? You must see how wrong this is!* The fiery darts were piercing my heart as if parts of me were dying inside. I became confused, especially while I was seeing someone. In one way the relationship was a sense of solace yet in another way it welcomed a different kind of threat.

The Bible scriptures were still a refuge for me at times of fear and emotional anguish. One particularly painful evening, I knew I was about to give up on God's justice after Scott's mental attack on me. I begged God to speak through scripture to show me He cared about the wrong being done to me by Scott. I opened the bible expecting a direct message of refuge from my anguish. The first thing I read came from 2 Samuel 2:9 KJV, "He will keep the feet of His saints, and the wicked shall be silent in darkness; for by strength shall no man prevail." The scripture gave me hope that this would not destroy me and one day he would be silenced. Just as Christ suffered at the hands of wicked people, I would have to trust that His grace would get me through as well.

"So then, faith comes by hearing and hearing
by the word of God."
Romans 10:17 NKJV

Throughout the following months, unbelief regularly knocked on my heart's door. I wondered if God even cared about what was happening. *Why should I care so much about pleasing God when He seems to be doing nothing about my pain? Why try so hard? Look where it brought me. I should just do whatever I feel like doing.* I was just too weak to press on like I once had. I was getting so weary; I failed to put on my spiritual armor because I was not eager to battle much longer. My nerves couldn't take any more. I felt forsaken.

Over the next year, I had compromised my relationship with my Heavenly Father. I was crossing lines in my own personal life substituting them for my intimacy with God. I was definitely feeling weak in the faith, selfish and sorry for myself. Even though my flesh was weak, I still inched my way forward, still going to church. I still had a mustard seed of faith to believe this was just my rough season.

> *"For I do not understand my own actions. For I do not do what I want, but I do the very thing I hate. Now if I do what I do not want, I agree with the law, that it is good. So now it is no longer I who do it, but sin that dwells within me. For I know that nothing good dwells in me, that is, in my flesh. For I have the desire to do what is right, but not the ability to carry it out. For I do not do the good I want, but the evil I do not want is what I keep on doing. Now if I do what I do not want, it is no longer I who do it, but sin that dwells within me."*
>
> *Romans 7:15-20 ESV*

Over a year of dating Tom, I was beginning to feel stuck in a relationship that wasn't lining up with all I had dreamed. Yes, I was lonely, hurt and had fears about the future. I diverted to a relationship for a sense of comfort and attention, subtly letting my guard down. This relationship was not the best example for my children either. I had compromised and I started to feel entangled in the relationship, so I prayed for guidance. Thankfully in my time of confusion, a friend and sister from church, Tracey Guilbeault, lovingly shared her concerns about the path I was on. This only confirmed what I knew in my heart I needed to do. The right thing to do was break off the relationship. Tom wasn't the person I could see myself with. We were two lonely people, but not on the same path. I felt bad that it saddened him, but I had to get real with God with my whole heart.

I thought about some of the poor decisions I had been making over the last few years: *Had I been too generous out of a lack of value for myself? Was I in such a bad emotional state that I was willing to put others' needs even above my own or, for that matter, my children's? What was I thinking? I couldn't blame anyone but myself, I allowed all of this!* As I pondered my poor choices, from the people I had been given myself to, to financial mistakes, I became angry with myself. The more I gave others, the more pain I brought upon myself! I realized I had been justifying my actions because I had so much disappointment, rejection, despair and grief afterwards. Helping people didn't help me or make me more valuable. I had believed a lie.

> *"If we confess our sins, He is faithful and just to forgive us our sins and to cleanse us from all unrighteousness."*
> *1 John 1:9 ESV*

Busyness, negative thoughts, and compromise kept me from educating and nurturing myself. It was like I got lost in a dark fog during that time. My convictions had subtly diminished over the past years, hindering my own growth. I had lost the ability to be in control, allowing others to affect my life. From now on, I would stand up and set boundaries, standards and goals for myself and my daughters' futures.

There was one positive insight I learned about myself. My actions proved that I'd finally been real enough to let my own guard down and stopped pretending I have it all together. That alone was a huge milestone for me and different territory, allowing the *wrong* path to comfort my weary soul. I was always the one who did things right but I'd become weak instead of strong. For once in my life I stopped caring what people thought which was, in a weird sense, healthy. I knew that Christ Himself was the only One who understood my betrayal and I knew He forgave me which was all that mattered. My mistakes are forgiven. I was worthy of forgiveness regardless of my weakness. I came boldly to the throne of grace because I became the one who needed mercy now. God met me right where I was at, just as

He would with others who struggle with their desires. Perhaps that was what I needed to learn through it all. I would keep this truth as anchor from this point on.

"This hope is a strong and trustworthy anchor for our souls. It leads us through the curtain into God's inner sanctuary."
Hebrews 6:19 NLT

Actualizing Your New Truth
Key Points

Recognizing the Drive to Strive

"The better you know yourself, the better the relationship with the rest of the world."
Toni Collette

Codependents don't know what valuable feels like. They try to fix or help people in the guise of loving them in order to feel valued. They sometimes settle for less than God's best. Unaware of the prison of fear or shame that's driving them, they fail to set higher standards for their lives. This is often why they don't have firmer boundaries. If emotions surface, they may silence them automatically in order to keep peace and maintain a sense of value. It is as if their essence is asleep in order to keep some sort of functionality in their lives and relationships.

Re-evaluating your Core Beliefs

"We change our behavior when the pain of staying the same becomes greater than the pain of changing. Consequences give us the pain that motivates us to change."
Henry Cloud

Those of us who have been abused may feel we were not worthy of God's best especially as hurtful words pierce the soul again. There may be a deep mental stronghold from early childhood in need of healing. It is difficult for a frozen essence to grasp the depth of His love because it's never been felt or experienced at an intimate level. Some people can't receive His free gift of love and forgiveness so they continue to strive to be right in all they do to feel better about themselves. Some can't forgive themselves for poor choices, so their self-punishment results in limitations. Not knowing the truth of our value is one of the root causes of depression, anxiety and a lack of boundaries. We need to be willing to examine why we have these defeating and self-sabotaging beliefs. As His beloved child, we can train our brain to accept our value to Him. Listen to Him say: *Come, let me love you, I gave my life to you.*

> *"Cease striving and know that I am God."*
> *Psalm 46:10 NASB*

God wants you to communicate with Him. Tell God what you feel about your pain and talk about why it hurts. Listen for His voice by reading scriptures, opening up to a trusted believer or listening to worship music. Let Him reveal how He desires to restore you. Imagine a happy ending to your story. The places that made you fear are places He will make you strong. That was the reason He died; to redeem you from the consequences of sin. Imagine Jesus, who knew exactly how it felt to be wronged as you were as a child. Then imagine Him comforting you and leading you through to a beautiful, peaceful and safe place. This helps you connect again to your wounded essence and the Father who cares about your feelings. He holds nothing against you for wrong choices and cares only that you become whole. Listen more to His scriptural promises, instead of rehashing problems, and make those promises your new truth. Meditate on them. Speak them out loud so that your brain literally hears your own voice. The gates of Hell cannot prevail. Those scriptures are God's words therefore demon forces begin to shut down and fade away. Put on the robe of righteousness as His child. Spiritual chains begin to literally fall off as they no longer keep you captive as you know to whom you belong. Light is putting out darkness. You are gaining spiritual ground. Continue to own these truths so that the lies you believed as a child become silenced. You are building healthy pathways of neurons in your brain. This will soon change your whole paradigm as grace and love overflows in your soul.

Believe you are worthy of love and of His power to work mightily in your life, just as you were as an innocent child. Expose the lies and confront them with the truth and love you now know, which disables the negative mental strongholds. Allow His kingdom to come and His will to be done by trusting in His promises.

"For the weapons of our warfare are not of the flesh but have divine power to destroy strongholds."
2 Corinthians 10:4 ESV

Go deep with God. Scripture states that "deep calls unto deep" in Psalms 42:7. He draws near to you as you draw near to Him. As you do, emotional freedom and maturity will come naturally, restoring your true essence as He predestined.

When tempted to compromise our feelings or values, we can easily default to our old habitual patterns. If you succumb to that familiar place, be aware of your feelings. Put unhealthy thoughts captive to the truth. Put on your spiritual armor for the battle of your mind. Read Ephesians 6:10-18. Once you learn to protect your own mind, you can better protect yourself within your relationships. The freedom to speak your thoughts leads to greater fulfilment in every area of your life.

"Keep thy heart with all diligence for out of it flows the issues of life."
Proverbs 4:23 KJV

Speak Out and Use Boundaries

If your spouse or children have a pattern of abuse or irresponsibility, don't cave under their manipulation or make excuses for their wrong behavior. Unconditional love does not mean being a doormat. Our boundaries help us care for ourselves and help us be more effective. It doesn't mean you are uncaring. It can mean you are committed to the relationship enough to explain your feelings. You love them enough to speak the truth, even if they don't want to hear it. If it's easier, communicate with them in writing. Healthy boundaries allow the other person to grow in empathy toward others. Boundaries move others to do what's right, which may lead them to grow emotionally and press them to examine why they do what they do. Because of you they may become influenced to surrender their self-centered ways and grow up. These are emotionally stretching yet maturing practices for both parties. This can provide you with a peace inside that you are doing right. In your heart you know it, so begin listening to the right voice.

It's imperative that the person crossing your boundary knows that there is a line there. You have the right to speak your mind in a respectful manner. If that line has been made clear and it continues to be violated or minimized, then greater actions may be necessary. Intimidation or manipulation from others may require some tough love on your part, just by saying no. Some people need to learn that the world does not revolve around them and their childish behavior. If they get abusive or you are not comfortable to move forward with them, love yourself enough by removing yourself from the situation. If you are not safe call the police. You cannot love a person enough to make them change. Bullies need to learn to own their problems, consequences and choices, not you. You are not their savior. You are doing them a disservice by silencing yourself, keeping them from maturing.

> *"It is good for me that I have been afflicted;*
> *that I might learn thy statutes."*
> *Psalm 119:71 KJV*

Emotional Self-care

> *"But the helper the Holy Spirit, whom the Father will send*
> *in my name, He will teach you all things, and bring to your*
> *remembrance all that I said to you."*
> *John 14:26 ESV*

We are the stewards of our own lives. Changing old patterns will change our future through the seasons of life. The more we live within our true essence, the easier we recover lost emotions from our past, connecting their meaning for the future. This will develop maturity in every area of life. Christ gave us a masterful model of influence, power and love. He didn't let anyone get in the way of His mission. He taught people how to manage their lives so that the world couldn't manage it instead. He had to have strong boundaries to accomplish His vision and so should we. Here are some examples:

- Don't feel guilty saying no if you need to be taking care of yourself
- Allow others to take ownership of their problems
- Define your personal obstacles and set up a plan to address them
- Use your emotional triggers as a positive guide without repressing them
- Don't let others push you into their plans for you, while negating yours
- Find and use your own thoughts and voice; share your true self with others
- Schedule time to do things you enjoy, which quiets your mind and feed your soul with scripture
- Exercise self-respect and don't reject support and compliments
- Expand your own growth and learn something new
- Discover your passions and an assignment God has for you
- Surround yourself with people who you respect and want to be like
- Be accountable to a wise person who is willing to guide your soul
- Be the real you, accepting that you don't have it all together all the time
- Forgive and show compassion and mercy to yourself

"You keep him in perfect peace whose mind is stayed on you, because he trusts in you."
Isaiah 26:3 ESV

Our essence grows by an inseparable connection with a holy God and a spirit-led relationship with Him. He will use people to help you, but use discernment to protect your growth. Don't let assumptions, fears or distortions override the truth within you. They may run you off course, allowing others to hijack your emotions again. Keep your emotions aligned with your vision for the future and be vigilant over your calling. No matter what your goals are, the use of healthy boundaries sets you up for success. Guard your heart be fully present, and protect your true essence from toxicity.

> *"Casting down arguments and every high thing that exalts itself against the knowledge of God, bringing every thought into captivity to the obedience of Christ."*
> *2 Corinthians 10:5 NKJV*

Chapter 19

No More Limitations

"No, dear brothers and sisters, I have not achieved it, but I focus on this one thing: Forgetting the past and looking forward to what lies ahead."

Philippians 3:13 NLT

IT WAS MY thirty-eighth birthday. I was at the beauty salon doing Louise Quinlan's hair. She often came in with a story from the Bible or something she wanted to share with me about God. This particular day, she brought up the story of the man at the Pool of Bethesda in the bible. This man had an infirmity for thirty-eight years. Jesus was healing people at the pool and the man complained that nobody would help him and people were preventing him from getting into the pool for his physical healing. Jesus responded saying, "It has been done unto you. Just take up your mat and walk!" (John 5:8) The man did just what he said and was healed. It wasn't that Jesus wouldn't heal him. It was up to the man to stop complaining and start believing in order to receive his healing. Louise turned her head around and intently looked at me and said, "Don't you think thirty-eight years is long enough?" I told Louise that it was my thirty-eighth birthday and that she was speaking directly to me. It's not that God was withholding his promises from me; just as the man at the pool, I didn't have the insight to receive them. I couldn't see I was worth His love.

This confirmed to me that God was trying to open my eyes to see the lies I had believed about myself and God. I had to come to the point that I was tired of complaining to God about my life. I had to choose to believe that what God said was the truth, even if I felt unworthy. His blessings for my life are not out of my reach. It's up to me to receive them and it's that simple. I am worthy of His blessings. I thought about the thirty-eight years of darkness and wasted time, just like the Israelites wandering in the wilderness, complaining along the way to the Promised Land. My life was as if I was lost in a wilderness experience. Finally after forty years in the desert, the Israelites entered into their Promised Land. Wow. I'm so done being lost, hurt and taken advantage of! I am changing the way I think of myself and my future! I will begin to thank God starting today that by the time I have my fortieth birthday, I want to experience the freedom of living in my own Promised Land! Never mind waiting until eternity for my reward. He promised us heavenly blessings here on earth. I just never could see that until now! The limitations I had in my life were because of my own thinking. I was grateful for this life-altering lesson.

I would no longer see my past as a failure. I chose to look at it as experience that has turned to wisdom. It was as if shame was no longer a driving force behind my dreams and actions. Faith began to take its place as I believed that God does love me for who I am, even though I've missed the mark in so many ways. In fact, He knew why I missed the mark. I asked God to recompense me for my suffering starting now. It was neither fair nor easy having been forsaken by both parents and a husband. God said that He would not forsake me. All of these people are those who sought their own desires at my emotional expense. Why wouldn't God be compassionate toward me for the betrayal from the very people who should have loved me? I opened my heart to be fully known to Him, because I now could trust Him in every single area of my life.

I realized that over the last sixteen years, without knowing, I had let confusion, doubt and fear remove me from the first intimate connection I had when I first gave my heart to Jesus.

Trust had to go deeper, into the hurt I had as a child. I finally was back to that safe place, experiencing oneness with God, which filled me again with truth and hope. I believed that nothing could separate me from His love for me.

I began to love my life on my own with my kids. I would not take anything but His best from now on. I no longer would compromise out of fear in any way. I found myself to be right where God wanted me to be. There was a sweet peace in this place. Why mess with such a good thing? Right here and now I felt we had all we needed. I knew that one day the girls would see a healthy and respectful relationship in their lives, by which they would model their own. God knew my heart and vision for that becoming a reality. In the meantime there was a satisfaction in the intimate connection I had with Him.

I was feeling personal freedom again in my life. My mind was clearer and I truly felt grateful for all I'd been through and was learning about myself. There was no longer this invisible idol in my life that I was in pursuit of, that dream to have a family and live happily ever after. I trusted all of that into God's hands to deliver us in His timing. I had survived the loss of my dream to a hellish nightmare that came true. I still had lots of life ahead to live, now that I was finally at a time that I was okay with me. I was alone but I didn't feel lonely. I saw the purpose in the pain that brought me to this place of peace. I felt valuable to God and knew He would guide me from here.

My relationship with my dad had become better than ever and I was totally free from any oppression, fear or disappointment from our relationship. During my earlier years of marriage, at a time when I was seeking personal freedom from my past, I gave him the ultimatum of charges against him if he chose not get counselling to understand the extent of my suffering as a child. This confrontation was difficult but essential for my growth and his accountability back then. He did go for counselling and took full responsibility for his actions. He had made progress over time in his relationships and I was happy for him. Our talks became more meaningful. He told me that he wished he could have done things differently, admitting to the many poor choices with great regret. I was no longer hindered by his choices, which allowed me to be confident just being me.

If I spoke my mind, he would listen and even apologize. When I told him about Scott and I divorcing, he cried with me, held me and told me how sorry he was for me. I continued to use wise boundaries yet I could still allow our relationship to grow. I was free to live happy even if my dad was not where I wanted him to be in life. The past was not good but the future was still unwritten.

"And we have known and believed the love that God has for us. God is love, and he who abides in love abides in God and God in him."
1 John 4:16 NKJV

No More Limitations
Key Points

For my yoke is easy and my burden is light."
Matthew 11:30 NIV

The Peril of Perfect

Perfection can be a state in which few of us feel we've arrived. Imperfection always keeps us under the mark. Our culture taught us to strive for perfection to attain positive results. The fear of failure and rejection can easily become our driver as we fear man's opinion of us. Feeling unworthy because of self-imposed limitations, only amplifies the feeling that attaining God's very best is always out of your reach. Hopelessness and despair are evil tools of the enemy, leading people to frustration and depression.

I often felt responsible for the outcome, independent of help as if the outcome was due to only my efforts. Doing my best was not good enough and discounted. Fear of failure always haunted me. Our own beliefs hold us back from experiencing the truth of our worth to God. He does not change how we think, we do. With mindful meditation on truths from scripture, we can reconstruct our thoughts which eventually expose our own self-sabotaging, negative mindsets and limiting beliefs. Most of our obstacles are within our own minds.

Christ alone was perfect. We press toward that mark, but it's by His grace the Holy Spirit sanctifies us, uniting His perfection through our obedience. That's the incarnate work of Christ in us, our only hope for glory. See John 17:22.

The only opinion that truly matters is how God sees us. God wants to see you clothed in Jesus's righteousness, not our own. Have you molded your own perfection into His? If so, we insult the gift of His grace. "We love because He *first* loved us" (1 John 4:19 ESV). Our perfection must first come from His love for us and then our love for Him. It never works the other way around. It's not about what we do, it's about how we respond to what He has done for us.

When scripture refers to the word *perfect*, we must not misunderstand its meaning. It is not perfectionism as the world understands, but purity of heart and the grace to be a vessel of His perfection. He believes the best about us, so He can handle the worst in us. As His vessels we are being made complete, pure and holy. This in turn brings Him honor as we recover our true essence, which easily gets lost because of sin. His law is perfect so as we walk in His grace and truth, our essence becomes perfected and our soul expresses His work in us. This must become an anchor of truth in our soul. His word says, "We shall know the truth and the truth shall set us free" (John 8:32).

> *"Do not conform to the pattern of this world, but be transformed by the renewing of your mind. Then you will be able to test and approve what God's will is, his good, pleasing and perfect will."*
> *Romans 12:2 NIV*

Growth in Change

Negative experiences have the power to define you, destroy you or strengthen you. You will become a victim or a victor depending on the choices you make. The older you get, change becomes more difficult. Our controlled routines seem safer and more predictable, but are they bringing out the best possible outcome? Being tested by fire helps you to know who you really are and who you are not. You must lose your old life to find your new one, then live within a higher truth. God's promises must be tested so we can learn to validate them. It states in John 16:13 that "the spirit of truth will guide us into all truth and show us things to come" (paraphrased).

Early patterns of thought can be so deeply ingrained, especially when we've learned a sense of personal validation from them. This *conditioned* sense of value inhibits our security in being our powerful and authentic selves even in our imperfections. God didn't say love your neighbor *better* than yourself! He said that you shall love your neighbor as yourself (Mark 12:31 KJV). In taking care of yourself, you may actually be exercising the power over darkness.

Challenge yourself to create neural pathways in your brain and strengthen your faith muscles by reading inspiring scripture suited for your growth. Speak out loud words of truth about yourself and your future. There is spiritual power that accompanies the inspired words of God. You will begin to attract good things and your energy will become more powerful and effective. Your pain was meant for a great purpose. Everything Satan made for bad, God wants to make for good. You've been given victory over this battle.

"Blessed is the one who perseveres under trial because, having stood the test, that person will receive the crown of life that the Lord has promised to those who love Him."
James 1:12 NIV

A Renewed Mind

"Seek ye first the kingdom of God and all these t hings shall be added unto you."
Matthew 6:33 KJV

God's heart is motivated by love for you. As you grow in this truth, your life will change automatically because His kingdom is within His children. (Luke 17:21 KJV). The outcome of your life is no longer fear-led, but love-led. Therefore, failure, shame or rejection do not rule your life. You live on a higher paradigm which allows God to use you as an extension of His hand. Where God guides, He will provide. Since most of your battles started in your mind, pray for wisdom and direction, clothing yourself in spiritual armor and the mind of Christ. See Ephesians 6:11-18 and 1 Corinthians 2:16.

Position yourself for your destiny to unfold. Tap into your God-given potential and watch how God gets involved as you become intimate with Him. Make this your new passion so that bad habits don't creep in again. Create a vision of where you want this all to go. The Bible states: "Where there is no vision the people perish: but he that keepeth the law, happy is he" (Proverbs 29:18 KJV). Herein you are operating in the perfect law of love, under the perfect parent in your recovered essence. Just as Jesus obeyed, you will more freely follow Him in your renewed mind.

There will be a freedom to love, even after what others have done to you. The fact you can love after pain is God's redemptive power alive in both your essence and redeemed soul, allowing a part of heaven to touch earth through grace. Your past pain becomes a gift from God to others. Your influence through Christ has a profound effect because of His love flowing in and through you. Your redeemed essence holds on to the grace which is also offered to those in need. Since you received it for yourself, people may sense something different about you because you are a vessel containing His love.

As you grow in this intimacy with your Father through the Holy Spirit's leading, you begin to envision the mantle He has given you. You will leverage your calling with the resources He brings to you. It's important to physically position yourself for the next move of God on your life. The bible states that your steps are ordered by God, so don't move ahead, but be in step with Him (Psalm 37:23). You may experience dreams or thoughts that repeatedly come to mind that bear witness inside you about what to do. You are learning to listen to His voice in your gut so your intuition becomes sharper. Heaven's perception is reaching yours. Your pain is converging with your purpose and God is about to bring a supply to see it come to pass. As the wind cannot be stopped by man, you become moved by the flow of His Spirit without fearing the influences of the enemy. You begin to access the mysteries of His kingdom.

> *"Therefore if anyone be in Christ, he is a new creature, old things are passed away, behold all things are become new."*
>
> *2 Corinthians 5:17 KJV*

Chapter 20

The Divine Connection

IT WAS LIBERATING to feel good about myself and like who I was becoming. Even my relationships became richer because I was okay being me. In fact, it seemed to free others to open up and be who they really were. I had learned more about God's mercy for all my bad choices, which in turn helped me to express a deeper mercy towards others, yet in a non-enabling way. The grace to love people without fear or pride could only come from Him. I sensed a love within me which gave me a kind of inner confidence I had never known. It was as if shame and fear had no influence on me any longer. My brain literally began to function better and my mind was much clearer.

As I became emotionally better, I was more energetic, patient and creative with my daughters. I was able to give them much more of my time, energy and love. God had taken us through so much. I wondered how the past thirteen years went by with me trying to parent without any idea of what a healthy upbringing looked like. They had so much loss to deal with— their Grandmother dying so young and their Daddy not living in the family home. But we were not alone. We shared our home with our cat, two pugs and their eight puppies. We took in a Panamanian student from the St. College Homestay Program, which was a great experience. We enjoyed our neighborhood and frequent walks through the wooded trails to Seven Hills and the river alongside the woods. There was a familiar peace enjoying those simple moments of God's presence in the beauty of nature. It reminded me of the peace I felt on the farm as a child and I was grateful the girls could enjoy this too.

I made it a priority to take better care of myself and began running. As I ran, I meditated on the scriptures: "...let us also lay aside every weight, and sin which clings so closely, and let us run with endurance the race that is set before us, looking to Jesus the founder and perfecter of our faith, who for the joy that was set before him endured the cross, despising the shame, and is seated at the right hand of the throne of God" (Hebrews 12:1-2 ESV).

I emptied the house of all unnecessary items, especially those that kept me in the past. It was time to move forward. I understood more clearly how my daunting past affected me and how I allowed fears to affect my marriage and my life. I felt whole and complete, even without a man in my life. I had no emptiness or longing inside, happy to use my energy and time for my daughters and me. It was actually liberating to give God first place in my life. We were safe in His perfect will. I trusted He knew what was best for us and would see us to a much better future.

It became easier to discern the signs of a false identity in a person, remembering how I once was subliminally attracted to it. God gave me eyes to see things that I couldn't see before as the veil of darkness had been lifted, just as the scriptures state. I was thankful for my past for all that I was learning on the other side of the pain. When I encounter the man God has in store for us, I would still be able to love, even after all that I had gone through. God did that miracle in my heart. I was not going to withhold my respect and love from a good man because of my negative experiences. My daughters will see what a healthy relationship looks like and how to be treated. This time, I will be sure, without question. I began a list of what I'd like in a man:

- Must accept and love my daughters and actively involve them
- He loves adventure and the outdoors
- Pleasant disposition and great communication
- Honest and open about what he's feeling

- Has sense of purpose and a strong work ethic without frequently complaining about it
- He has a sense of purpose and respectful leadership style modeling self-disipline
- Spiritually we connect deeply
- Has good values and convictions yet is not legalistic
- Has enough life experiences; owns his mistakes
- Knows how to have a good laugh and have fun
- He's courageously strong yet tenderhearted and patient
- Treats me like I'm his cherished and only woman
- Talks about his day and wants to know all about mine
- Regularly offers to help and serve

I was seeing the name *Wilson* on trucks as they passed by. This was also the encryption on the basketball from years ago. It was hard to forget that night God spoke to me about His promise, still active and remaining, for the right one to come into my life.

Wilson might appear on singles websites, I thought. Wouldn't that be like God, to give me a clear direction by showing me that name in order to lead me to my new husband? It seemed fitting to what the paradox represented even though it seemed childish to believe such. I was reminded that God keeps His promises and since I have faith as a child, why not believe? I was open to God using the Internet since I could screen profiles according to faith, age, location, status and interests as long as I was discerning and was guided by His wisdom to proceed. I searched for months and never came across one with the name *Wilson*.

I began to imagine a relationship with someone I could respect and admire who was genuine and wise. I imagined being treated like a lady and thought about what it would be like to feel cherished and understood deeply. For once in my life I would learn what it feels to be the recipient of the same love and respect that I gave. Wow, imagine that, being an equal! I tried to get my head wrapped around that fact. It was like I never even gave something that simple even a thought! I wasn't expecting perfection, but someone who was truly committed, hardworking, who loved people and was willing to learn and grow into their fullest potential. I saw myself and my daughters as worthy recipients of this kind of love, after all that we had been through. I would never settle for less ever again.

> *"Who will separate us from the love of Christ? Will tribulation, or distress or persecution, or famine, or nakedness, or peril or sword? But in all these things we overwhelmingly conquer through Him who loved us."*
> *Romans 8:35, 37 NASB*

I knew in my heart and mind that this was the state of mind in which people needed to be before a relationship with someone turns into commitment. A secure person will be discerning enough to recognize another secure person. They are free to share their thoughts and are interested in the thoughts and feelings of another. They understand where the lines of control should be and what to leave in God's hands. They've learned about the grace of God enough to suffer well through the battles of life and have the scars and lessons to prove it. They are walking in the light of God's truth.

I ended my membership to Match.com, but I was still able to search profiles without making contact. I browsed every month or so, enough time to populate some new profiles. Over the last few years I'd opened hundreds of profiles. I still had a sense that God may bring the name *Wilson* up on one of them.

One day, there it was: *Wilson* was part of a profile name on Match.com! My heart began to pound in my chest. I calmed myself down before I took a closer look. I said to myself, *what are the chances? Don't get your hopes up high. I may find him unattractive or wrong for me.* His profile picture was a distant one and I could barely distinguish his face. *Hmm, he's probably not too handsome if he doesn't want to show himself up close. I would be fine with someone average looking. Looks mean so much less to me now.* I continued to read his information and I liked his profile otherwise. He wrote in a way that gave me more understanding of the depth of person he was. *He seems wise and communicates like he has a purpose. I like that.* All the other important criteria matched as well. His height, weight, age, interests and faith were fine except for one negative thing; he lived two hours away, in Michigan. Well, I thought, it's harmless to send him a "wink" and maybe even a note to ask him if he has other pictures of himself.

After a couple of days I noticed he responded. I opened his note and he had not yet changed or added a better picture. His note was polite and he asked for my e-mail address to continue correspondence and to send me a clearer picture of himself. His name was Malcolm. I gave him my email address. When his email came through, the Wilson name was in the address. I opened his email and before I opened the attachment, my heart began to pound again. I looked at the picture of what looked like his two kids and him. I was very impressed with what I saw. *Wow,* I thought, *he is so handsome! I love his eyes and even the sincerity in them.* I stared at the picture for a while, wondering if I was looking at my future husband.

I reminded myself to not read into or overanalyze things, even though everything about this encounter matches up so far with what God had showed me about five years ago. It all originated from that dark night, after desperately waiting for an answer about my failing marriage. God used the wind to roll the *Wilson* ball, causing it to stop in front of me to confirm that His promise for a blessed marriage remained true. I was comforted in knowing He would unveil its full meaning after I had questioned what the two bouquets represented to my life. He showed me then; He would one day connect my path with a very special man in His timing, not mine. This would confirm the coincidental paradox of the two bridal bouquets at two separate weddings and what they represented in my life: The first bouquet toss caused me pain and humiliation, an allegorical representation of my first marriage. At another wedding, as I stood far away from the bouquet toss to avoid a similar experience, the second bouquet was miraculously struck by the ceiling fan, in the opposite direction, landing at my feet. I knew in my heart that someday, the fulfilment this promise from God would be unveiled, representing the meaning of second bouquet. I knew that God's faithfulness to me would be revealed through the name *Wilson* because of that night.

I was astounded at the thought that this could be the

promise from God I'd been waiting for. If things did continue, I should not be surprised. I knew what God spoke deep into my heart back then and I held on to His promise for what it meant. Perhaps this is the day it begins.

We exchanged phone numbers to make our communication easier. We talked quite a lot about our lives, what we learned, our values and what we were passionate about. He communicated so well and seemed so wise, caring and gentlemanly. Every conversation was deeply meaningful and so enjoyable, never boring. Our interests and goals were so similar. We both loved the outdoors, exercise and adventure. After over a month of feeling good about everything so far, I was ready to meet him in person. We planned to meet at Great Lakes Crossing.

I walked in to find the location where we agreed to meet. I didn't see him there. I continued walking and discretely looking around, hoping I would see him first so I could watch him. I wore my hair wavy, unlike the photos, so that he may not recognize me first. I turned around to walk back to the meeting spot and still didn't see him. I stopped and wondered, *which way do I go now? If he sees me now, I obviously look lost.* Then I saw him standing with his hand slightly raised and waving and a smile on his face. He wore a goatee, unlike his shaven face in the picture he sent. *He's very handsome,* I thought. We walked toward each other and greeted with a hug.

We had a nice dinner at a restaurant nearby. I held back from revealing what I sensed God was unveiling to me. He was so easy to talk to and very much a gentleman. I felt so comfortable that I had to try to keep from saying so much in one night. There would be plenty of time to spread our talks out more in the future, that is, if he was still interested. I asked him questions, remembering the criteria I had to see in someone before moving forward. His answers were very sincere and definitely not crafty, vague or unsettling in any way. I couldn't see anything that I didn't like about him.

We left the restaurant and walked toward the entrance. I brought my camera with me, just in case. I courageously pulled it out and asked someone nearby to take a picture of us. Afterward he walked me to my car. I wasn't quite sure how he was feeling about the evening, since his demeanor was very calm, controlled and polite. He asked if he could call me soon. I responded, "I'd love that!"

As I drove home, which was forty minutes or so from the border, the song by Delirious, "Rain Down," began to play. The words, "Give me the strength to cross this water, keep my heart upon your altar," and the chorus, "Do not shut the heavens, but open up our hearts; rain down, rain it down on me." I sobbed with joy and awe of what I sensed God had done on this day, opening up heaven, pouring down His blessing in my life. I danced in the seat of my car to the song, picturing Jesus dancing and celebrating with me as blessings from heaven began to pour on my life.

I was attracted to everything about Malcolm. I tried to find something that wasn't right, because I knew I would never compromise again; I felt only peace. I then thought about the blending of our families and the conflict that could bring. *What about the two different countries we live in?* We would just have to take it one step at a time.

Distance was a good thing. It forced us to have further discussions about our individual goals, our priorities, and the things we valued about relationships. We both learned a great deal from our failed marriages, what we did wrong and what to do right. We discussed our perceptions of faith and its value to us. He also had some negative experiences with church people but that didn't change his strong relationship he still had with God and his commitment to serve Him. I liked that he was balanced and discerning, knowing the difference between religion and an authentic relationship with God. I admired that he liked to learn and grow to be all that he can be. We shared a common interest in mental health and psychology. He was working toward becoming a counselor. He was physically, mentally and spiritually appealing to me. I admired that he had a strong work ethic yet took time to enjoy life.

He loved his kids dearly and got emotional when he spoke about what they went through during the tough times in the marriage and through the divorce. He didn't give up on his marriage easily. As he talked about the marriage struggles, I knew he could relate to some of the challenges of mine. That was also very important to me.

He had a passion to learn and help others grow as well. He was attentive to what I thought and felt, which was so different for me. All of this made me more attracted to him. I knew that with all that I was seeing about this man, he was everything I wanted in a husband. He was committed, wise, honest, open, caring and, in my perception, deserved to be loved for the person he was. *Will I be that blessed woman to love and respect him like I feel he deserves?*

I knew I wanted to move forward in our relationship. He was showing more interest as well. He said that, right from the beginning, he had a green light about us. He did have one hesitation before we even corresponded. He admitted he was reluctant of the fact I lived in Canada and he would not feel comfortable leaving his stable job. He was still drawn to my profile and he chose to ignore the distance factor for now. God had divinely brought us together, so I believed, just as miraculously, He would somehow work out all the details ahead of us.

One day, while at his house, I was willing to be vulnerable. I finally felt the moment to unveil to him about my sacred events of the two bouquets and the moment God used the wind to send the Wilson ball that night while seeking God for answers. I wondered if he might find it silly, as some people may not relate to my child-like faith, especially intelligent people. He interpreted it exactly as I did and believed that God had given me this paradox, which led me to him. He was intelligent, but also a wise man, so I wasn't surprised that he appreciated my simple faith.

We bonded so easily, it was refreshing. His heart for God and his tender ways were like pieces of heaven unveiling something beautiful to me. We communicated so uninhibited, with depth and respect for one another. It deepened my attraction to him.

In the past I would listen to those wholesome love songs of the '70s and wonder if I would ever know the genuine love those artists expressed. I always felt I missed out on this blessing; but after we were brought together, every song began to resonate with my soul.

With this kind of foundation, we could face any challenge with faith and determination to pursue until we found clarity of

God's will. We had an advocate in each other, which would bring the out the best in us. We saw the prior damage to our hearts as lessons, not obstacles. We would use them to build a firmer foundation for those we would help someday.

Before I was free within my essence, I did everything I could to make someone else happy. Now I have someone to share life with to do what makes God happy. In doing so, we make each other happy too.

"The meeting of two personalities is like the contact of two chemical substances; if there is any reaction, both are transformed."
Carl Jung

The Divine Connection
Key Points

Recognizing Authenticity

When a person lives free from maladaptive beliefs, tangled emotions and confusing relationships, perceptions are so much clearer. Since they are no longer tainted with deception, they can be more authentic in their thoughts, actions and choices. The fruit of peace and the freedom to love reflects the maturity of a person's true essence.

Making a life-changing decision involving another should not be uncertain. You should have a confidence that *you know that you know* that you both have what it takes. There should be enough evidence to confirm the fullness of God's best is within view. You are not ignoring any red flags. You can discern if someone is genuinely caring and wise. They will complement your passion and destiny, equally partnering towards a shared vision. If not, it's as though something is incomplete in your gut that you might be ignoring. Think about this scripture and when we are connected to the truth, we are able to grow into our authentic and original design:

"I am the vine, you are the branches; he who abides in Me and I
in him he bears much fruit, for apart
from Me you can do nothing."
John 15:5 NASB

Marriage brings two people into one flesh. If you allow another person to be grafted into your life when they don't align with your destiny, your essence can become tainted. Those are branches that don't belong on the vine and simply cannot bear the fruit of true freedom through you. They become a life-draining burden to your soul and you should cut off (prune) the unhealthy soul ties with them. God's essence flows through you with peace when your deepest essence connects with another's authenticity. Your emotionally intimate relationship with each other reflects your intimate relationship with God as you knit your hearts together in one accord.

A Direct Connection to Love

Being authentically connected to God moves His heart to action. Coincidences may be a result of impressions on our hearts, which are converging with God's divine plan. He may speak to us in dreams and nudges as we seek His voice about the questions in life. He does want us intimately acquainted with His voice and longs for us to invite Him to get involved with our lives, especially where we need His help. Our prayers to Him can literally accelerate us toward our divine destiny. The words of your prayers actually affect the outcome of your life because you are connected to a divine purpose. The key is to pray according to His will. His divine intervention is physical proof of your intimate relationship with Him. He longs to fulfill His promises in our lives, but requires us to be an open vessel of faith to bring them to pass. It's so amazing that we can connect with the God of such power! Can your faith be childlike and simple enough to block out human logic or pride and allow the miraculous to unfold in your life?

"How abundant are the good things that you have stored up for those who fear you that you bestow in the sight of all, on those who take refuge in you."
Psalms 31:19 NIV

I want to mention to hopeful readers, who may use websites to find a match with someone—just because my matching experience worked for me, does not mean it will work the same way for everyone. Knowing God's voice takes discernment, clear confirmation and wisdom. Signs and signals alone are not your guidance. They can confirm purpose and destiny but are not meant to rescue unhealed emotions. Until you've cultivated a deep intimacy and know His voice from inside, you may think something is God's path when it may not be. Internet searches have been proven to be fatal! Be very cautious if you choose to use them! I'm advocating God's will in this book, not suggesting you should try online matching.

Chapter 21

True or Counterfeit Love?

GOD HAD CONFIRMED our destiny as one. We eventually began to blend our lives together. We had both been through so much and learned so much from our pasts. Blending our families would be a task but we would all get through it. I was confident and at peace that we were emotionally and spiritually equipped for the days ahead. I knew it would be difficult pulling my daughters away from their family, friends and community; in fact that was the hardest on me as well.

Marriage would begin the immigration process and the girls and I would become legal immigrants of the United States in about two years. We set a wedding date and planned a small reception and dinner at Spago's Italian Restaurant.

Nothing was going to stop what only God had put together. I still at times felt hurt by some of the harsh treatment that came through Scott but I had better things to focus on. I knew deep inside me that God did care enough to bless the girls and me so faithfully. Perhaps the move farther away was God's mercy on us.

I made a prayer request to God on our upcoming wedding day. It would be fitting for Him to do something that could only be from Almighty God. I asked Him for a sign, believing He was rejoicing for us over what I knew God had orchestrated in bringing Malcom and I together. After all, this marriage came about all because of two bouquets and a basketball, which I believed God was totally behind all along to guide my life to this point! This *God Smile* would confirm that He knew my heart; that I did follow his direction as I trusted in His promises that led me to this wedding day.

We had a small ceremony led by Pastor Luke and Leila, who knew me since I started attending Windsor Christian Fellowship back in 1986. Pastor Luke was always there to give out "Daddy hugs" over the years, and their ministry together touched many marriages in the church. It was nice to have them officiate. Malcolm not only said a vow to me but to Natasha and Jericka. It was hard for all of us to keep the tears back.

Throughout the day I had that faith-filled anticipation that, again, God cared about my heart's desire for the *God Smile* to be revealed, somehow. The dinner at Spago's was exceptional. Our private party room was the perfect size and we would soon open the divider to enjoy the other section of Spago's with the dance floor and the three-piece Italian band. My daughters were excited to get the dancing started. But first, Malcolm and I would have our wedding dance to the song by Natalie Grant and New Song, "When God Made You." As we danced, we knew that the words of that song were meant for us, reminding us of his faithfulness. My favorite line was when they sang, "Gone are all the questions about why; and I've never been so sure of anything in my life." Everything we both had gone through previous to this day prepared us for God's will; His very best. I reminded God as we danced that I was still welcoming His *smile* on this meaningful day.

When we finished, we stood waiting for the wooden divider wall to open, so that we could expand the fun and dancing into the other room. There were a couple of tables with dining guests against the opposite side, who probably would be surprised when the wall beside them started to rise up. As I stood before the disappearing wall, there sat two people directly in front of me, only about two feet away from where we stood. At that table sat Donna and Jeff Farron. Donna and I screamed with surprise as our eyes met! I was elated and hugged them both and realized at that moment I had received my *God Smile*. I got everyone's attention to make an announcement: "I asked God for His signature gift and smile on this day and here it is! The second wedding bouquet that landed at my feet was Donna's at their wedding! This is Donna, and here she is at my wedding! I hadn't spoken to her in years, but God saw that it was fitting for her to join our celebration of God's faithfulness to me. This is not just a coincidence; it is a smile from God to show me He was in it all along!"

"Let us hold fast the confession of our hope without wavering,
for He who promised is faithful."
Hebrews 10:23 KJV

True or Counterfeit Love?
Key Points

"Therefore what God has put together, let no man separate."
Mark 10:9 NIV

Raptured in Oneness

"To be loved and not known is comforting but superficial. To be known and not loved is our greatest fear. But to be fully known and truly loved is, well, a lot like being loved by God. It is what we need more than anything. It liberates us from pretense, humbles us out of ourself-righteousness and fortifies us for any difficulty life can throw at us."
Timothy Keller

We were made for great relationships including the one with Him. He delights in giving His children gifts, just as a loving parent would. God went out of His way, proving that the greatest acts of love came through His great sacrifice and empathy for mankind. That kind of love has the power to change hearts as we become one with Him.

Self-sacrificing love is trustworthy. His truth restores our essence to new life. His leadership style is higher than worldly kings. In Heaven and Earth, He rules as King of true love. Expressing gratitude for all He accomplished through His suffering satisfies the thirsting soul in a heartfelt exchange of love. He delights in our praise. He visits worship, becoming one in the Spirit with those who enter in to the inner sacred sanctuary. This intimate flow of energy lifts the delusions that creep into our minds. This is why many Christians feel compelled to worship Him. He deserves the praise for what He has already provided, so our faith also becomes restored in worship. This love exchange makes us feel more blessed to give than to receive. I'm sure it pleases His heart. It's so much more than knowing about Him. He has invited us into the mysteries of His Kingdom. Only those who are hungry for intimacy with Him are granted the privilege of knowing Him in this way. In turn, our soul prospers as we become one in our essence with Him. See 3 John 1:2.

As we get better acquainted with God and abide with Him, we allow His spiritual law of life and love to work through us. Just as a couple in love will court before their wedding day, you have an opportunity to get to know Christ through an intimate and very exciting relationship with Him until the day when the veil is lifted and we become fully known. Spend your valuable time here preparing for that special day when all who are His will be raptured into oneness with our Savior and King! We will get to celebrate the greatest marriage supper ever and party like crazy in the fullness of our essence. This life on earth was meant to prepare us for that great wedding when Christ, the bridegroom, returns for a pure and spotless bride, His church, who *know* they are His. Scripture states this to prepare us:

"Let us be glad and rejoice, and give honor to him
for the marriage of the Lamb is come, and wife
hath made herself ready."
Revelation 19:7 KJV

Deceptive Love

"But the natural man receiveth not the things of the spirit of
God, for they are foolishness unto him, neither can he know
them, because they are spiritually discerned."
1 Corinthians 2:14 KJV

Mankind is catching up through their logic that pure love works for people. There is more awareness today about emotional intelligence and creating leaders and teachers who can empathize and connect with those under them. God put that in us because He is relational. This should call us to more discernment about authentic character and motives of people, especially leaders. The source of true or deceptive love will confirm its origin by means of an authentic relationship with others and God. The face of love can be deceiving but when you understand pure love's origin, it's easier to discern the counterfeits. Not only does this apply within our relationships but also in a larger scope in this present world system. Sadly, many still reject its very author who fully embodied the highest of love and relationship principles, Jesus Christ.

There is a movement on earth which I believe is hijacking some of the fundamentals of love and natural laws that God has provided for us, especially as we see unexplained miraculous events in our lives. Some philosophies will even reference *Christ* but omit Jesus. Some will believe in Jesus that he was a great teacher, yet deny He is the only way to heaven. The deceiver himself uses half-truths to distract people from the person who should get the credit for them, God our heavenly Father and Jesus Christ. He was *love personified.*

The New Age Movement claims that mankind discovers their own divinity using the powers of the universe to create your own reality. This way there is no ultimate moral standard to be accountable to, therefore excuses certain behavior out of preference because of the claim that it works for them. Each person validates his own self-centered experience creating their own truth to suit their emotional needs. Part of this is true as we are subject to spiritual laws as our carnal minds create our own *temporary* "reality". Moral Relativism changes over time as we gain experience and wisdom. The problem with moral relativism is that the concept of right and wrong has no place and there are no absolutes. So what happens when evil advances? How is mankind balanced if there is no conviction of sin? What about those who suffer as a result? Those of us who believe that sin separates us from a just God are accused of being *narrow minded.*

Relationships are the key to knowing and experiencing how His agape love works in us. Pure love requires obedience as well as love to operate in its fullness as Christ showed us in His intimate relationship with the Father. We obey out of love, not fear. This invokes agape love, a higher law of love than the law that New Agers and Universalists may feel comfortable with. It's not popular because of its sensual boundaries, so many pretend the law of sin and death doesn't have consequences. One day we will have to give account and choose to whom we give credit; to whom we belong and what we've done with the truth. Knowing truth will grow your essence and the lie will stifle it. There is a counterfeit for Jesus and his aim is to deceive you from being all you were meant to be.

"Jesus saith unto him, I am the way, and the truth, and the life: no one cometh unto the Father, but by me."
John 14:6 ASV

Relationships are ultimately where the heartbeat of love is expressed. Our interactions with people determine our spiritual and emotional maturity. It's important to recognize the motive behind what looks like love. The love motivated by self seeks its own way and lacks a desire for accountability to God which may be very appealing to those who believe in creating their own truth, making themselves God. Our childish instincts were to do our own will. To mature, we conform to Christ's likeness by the sacred virtues, which were meant to be imparted by our parents: trust and obedience. Jesus displayed the highest form of love to us and ultimately was accountable to God in whom He trusted. He had no selfish gain in mind for popularity or power, but only obeyed the Father through love and not fear. He gave us Jesus as our exemplar, His instructions, the gift of grace and His Holy Spirit who would guide us into all truth. He showed us how to engage the fullness of our essence and become powerful influencers and lovers of people.

Even America as a nation has lost touch with its roots, changed its relationships and therefore has changed its identity. It seems as though America is searching now more than ever for truth again. America needs to be rediscovered as a Christian nation, but it appears to be embracing half-truths. We must be cautious and mindful that those half-truths may be still connected to a terrible lie.

Without the incarnate nature of God through the risen Christ, mankind can function through a mental power that mimics traits of love, but at the core rejects the author of love. The person who refuses to give honor to God through His Son has likely built their lives outside of His sanctifying grace. If praise does not belong to God our Father and Christ our Savior, then who will receive the praise when it's all said and done? If a person desires the praise instead of God, then who might be behind that motive?

In my opinion, not standing up for the pure, innocent and abused should cause conviction in our hearts. I can understand people rejecting the poor examples of Christians, but I'm amazed at the flat out rejection and refusal of Christ's pure love for them after what He gave them. No person on earth has ever been able to match His expression of love. Christ never intimidated, rejected, deceived or abused anyone, but instead was innocent, conquered death for us, reassuring us of eternal life. Jesus was innocent yet was punished as if He was guilty. Many refuse to stand in the gap for Him and worship Him. Many are too busy creating their version of truth to suit their false self, rejecting the most valuable relationship available to restore their lost essence.

The counterfeiter of love, namely Satan, wants the praise to be taken from Christ because of pride. The accuser seeks to blame Christianity for the world's evils then he turns around with half-truths and similar principles that Christ taught, then will try to lead the world with them. He is so twisted, just like a master narcissist whom many are fooled by. In the long run, Satan was never looking out for the best interest of the people; only his own pride. What regret so many will feel when they realize the lies they believed. If they would only have loved in return the One who loved them the greatest. In a similar manner, some narcissistic people bring dishonor to others for selfish gain. They choose to diminish the selfless acts of love in others as if they were in vain. If you have suffered as a victim of such a person, Christ promises to recompense you in such a glorious way. He has already proven Himself faithful. He can and will satisfy your soul through the powerful gift of His grace.

"I will be glad and rejoice in your love, for you saw my
affliction and knew the anguish of my soul."
Psalm 31:7 NIV

False Light

"Woe to those who are wise in their own eyes
and clever in their sight."
Isaiah 5:21 NIV

The laws of attraction, high vibrational thoughts, higher consciousness and forces of light—it all sounds so positive and good. They exist because God created the laws of the universe and many people tapped into them, providing mankind with great inventions and theories. The highest laws of physics were vastly tapped into by Jesus Christ Himself. He connected to His Father, doing miracles as He converged with the heart of God's will. There are those who deny that Christ is the only mediator to God, yet still lust for the same power He operated in. Guess who's behind that goal.

"The god of this age has blinded the minds of the unbelievers,
so that they cannot see the light of the gospel that displays the
glory of Christ, who is the image of God."
2 Corinthians 4:4 NIV

New Age thinking was adapted from Eastern philosophies, which pull out similar laws, like sowing and reaping, yet are vastly different in origin. Some use channels, mediums and get messages from *angels of light*. They believe mankind is in ultimate control through their choices, which affect their karma, destiny and afterlife through their reincarnated beings. Any reference to God or the Cosmos or Higher power is always impersonal, without ultimate accountability, relationship or viable judgement because they want to *own* that. Because of this, they believe that their choices create their own heaven or hell on earth, calling on the universe to work for them. Instead of an intimate relationship with the person of God who created this universe with balance, they suggest that they are in control of their own truth, unyielding and disconnected from a very personal God.

As Christ-following believers begin to engage in the fullness of their true essence in these last days, converging their spiritual gifts and assignments with the heart and mind of God, we will see His manifest power in miracles. Many who recognize that anointing will flow with the Holy Spirit as He leads and will begin to flow in that power just as Christ said we would. We are seeing these bursts of revival and healings emerging. Satan hates the fact that Christ has greater power than he does. He did all he could to tempt Christ to fail just as he does with believers today.

Because he is jealous for attention, the Bible warns us that Satan will come as an angel of light. He will possess a person and assert his powerful *love* movement in the world with great eloquence. In that day, people's hearts will be full of fear; therefore many will embrace his intelligent words of light because of a need for peace in the world. His goal has been to remove Christianity altogether, and silence the Christians whom he hates and cause ill-informed people to hate them also. He will try to rule the world with a powerful solution of peace. Because of hidden pride, he lusts for the credit for his great philosophy and for implementing it into the world to control it from impending destruction. He will use his timely *new world order* as the only solution for the world; yet the degradation of mankind was because of his deceptive tactics to disregard the Holy Scriptures from the beginning. He was behind it all. Just when he reaches the point of removing God and scriptures from the constitution, schools, courts and nations, it seems to be perfect timing to turn himself in to the false hero he has been lusting to be all along (See Daniel 8:25). Be sure you give glory only to the One to whom it is due and heed biblical warnings of his deception, his greatest tool.

> *"And no marvel; for Satan himself is transformed*
> *into an angel of light."*
> *2 Corinthians 11:14 KJV*

Any area of human weakness will give Satan a foothold for deception in our lives. I have succumbed to deception much of my life out of false identity for mere acceptance and belonging. Any fear, pride or negative emotion that has never been surrendered to God can be subject to Satan's demise and deception. Many are proficient at creating such *light* without God. I'm amazed how deceiving pride can be. We have all been fooled by such a person. Some people appear too good to be true. Often it's because their core has been buried by a false identity fueled by fear or pride, controlled by the law of sin. Self-glorification and deception are means of attaining power to fuel their false self while their inner child remains abandoned. Some unrepentant souls end up in a state of reprobate where they are so blinded they have no conscience of guilt for their sin and its law in which they operate. In the King James Dictionary, reprobated refers to "abandoned to wickedness orto destruction." We all need to have our soul abandoned to God's *reconstruction.*

> *"This is what the Lord says: 'Cursed is the one who trusts in man, who draws strength from mere flesh and whose heart turns away from the Lord.'"*
> *Jeremiah 17:5 NIV*

Emptiness in the soul fuels a passion for it to be filled. When it's filled with healing from above, nothing compares. Complete healing has amazing benefits if it comes through the true healer. Every area of weakness is the perfect place for the light of redemption to do its perfect work, making us strong in His likeness. True satisfaction will come when we are fully engaging our true essence to love and be loved. Being real with others in a safe environment allows our pain to unite our humanity. Otherwise pain causes disconnect when it's used wrong.

If you reject God's love, you are embracing something that cannot match what God can do for you. Your essence remains lost and unredeemed. Don't hide your weakness but be real with the only person who knows everything about you. Open the door of your heart, reveal your inner self and let Him in. He can do the miraculous in and through you. Jesus himself said, "Very truly I tell you, whoever believes in me will do the works I have been doing and they will do even greater things than these, because I am going to the father." John 14:12 NIV

Love in a way that is not a waste, but love wisely and don't waste your love on selfish takers. Being loved and loving freely is a foretaste of heaven. The safety of God's love in you may bring the true person out in others. When you love people within the purity of your essence, you see the good in them, just as Jesus loved people. When you live free from the fear of rejection, you become free to be your authentic self, operating under an anointing of His power within you. Your life literally becomes the hands and feet of Christ through you as you grow in unity with the Father.

> *"Love the Lord your God with all your heart, and with all your soul, all your strength and with all your mind. And love your neighbor as yourself."*
> *Luke 10:27 NLT*

God's love always leads to restoration, life and hope. True love equals true life. Any life challenge that has been handed to us, no matter what it is, can bring something good from it over time when you let God in it. Nothing in this life compares to the suffering that Christ endured on the cross. Our suffering at the expense of others was the whole purpose for His sacrifice, out of pure love and compassion for us. He provided the way to redeem us from the pain and turn it into a purpose for which God would be glorified through us, just as Christ was glorified in the resurrection. That's why it's called the life blood; it brings us back to life. We can't make ourselves holy, but because of Christ's atoning and sanctifying love, we allow God to work His "magic" of grace through our surrender and obedience. Allow Him to work in your life, give Him the reigns and your life will never be the same. He always keeps His promises.

Chapter 22

True Love Keeps Promises

ANOTHER *GOD SMILE moment* came when Natasha won homecoming queen for Midland High in her senior year. It was the evening of the homecoming football game and the honoring of the king, queen and court. My dad made a point to attend for which I was so grateful. As the Midland High band played on the brightly lit up football field, I looked at my dad. Tears streamed down his face. I knew more was going on inside than I think he realized. For me, it was further closure from my past. I knew my dad was proud of me and my daughter Natasha, in her beautiful white homecoming gown, even though his words were not expressed. I was reminded of the little girl I once was, who wanted to be seen as his princess and adored. God was giving us both a piece of heaven, and simply put, it was a sign of God's goodness. I knew that I was restored from all pain from my childhood. Not only was my dad proud but I believe my Abba dad was too and that moment was another smile from heaven and closure from the past. Regardless of whether my dad and Scott saw us girls as the princesses we were, God our Heavenly Father sees us as such. We know who we are and to whom we belong. No longer should we have to prove ourselves worthy or strive for their love, because it dwells within us.

I've had many people ask questions like: "How can you let those who've hurt you back in you and your daughters' lives?"

Every one of us has caused someone to hurt at some point in life. I am very far from perfect. None of us have walked in the shoes of those who hurt us. We can still love them wisely, even from afar. It doesn't mean we put the innocent in harm's way. Loving in our strength does not mean we return foolishly to enabling or allowing children into a dangerous situation. We all need God's mercy. I've chosen to show it to others when it's welcome.

> *"We all, like sheep, have gone astray, each of us has turned to our own way; and the Lord has laid on him the iniquity of us all."*
> *Isaiah 53:6 NIV*

All sin is forgivable through the blood of Christ. His grace was given to us because He knew we cannot forgive deeply and then love deeply in our own strength. My sin is no less ugly in God's eyes compared to those who hurt me. If I was faced with the challenge, I believe that I was presented a choice to forgive. I felt compelled to love without fear instead and be strong in God's power. It's important to forgive the people who wounded you, but use God-given wisdom, even if you need to remain at a distance in order to be emotionally and/or physically safe. I remain careful in my relations with Scott and I still pray regularly for God to fully heal his wounds and all of the relationships involved. Scott has made some positive life changing choices and has thanked me for my forgiveness and understanding. This has been helpful to my daughters and me to see these changes in him.

I feel fortunate that my daughters and I have been able to navigate very rough waters. Understanding truth sets them free to be themselves, without taking on blame for their parents' problems. That has helped them recognize inherited tendencies, examine their hearts and discern unhealthy behaviors.

As my daughters matured, I told them some of the truths about the marriage failure in simple observant stages to the extent their age would comprehend without grief or confusion. Lying to children in order to protect the image of an abuser can cause them confusion. Loading them with information they can't comprehend is not good either. Children have a right to just be kids, not a parent's savior, partner or sounding board. So, when things were challenging in the relationship, the girls and I would discuss the matter, process it out and learn from it.

Since I could not change the outcome of the marriage, I looked to maximize this learning experience for them as something they would learn in life when they encounter similar people. They know to be watchful that some people may have unresolved issues or may have a behavioral or mental disorder. They understand that when another person cannot love them the way they would like, it is not their responsibility to *fix them* or strive for their acceptance, even from their father. That kind of love comes from their Father in heaven. They accept that reality and do not depend on an unmet dream like I did.

Today, Malcolm and I have an amazing marriage, friendship and ministry. Since we married, God has revealed His faithfulness in more ways than I imagined. As we encourage and support each other in our individual roles, we strengthen our bond together and with God. We are seeing the plans unfold in our business, Wilson Wellness Counseling, Coaching and Consulting and my Recovered Essence Programs. It is wonderful to love the true person he is and to know I am loved for the true person I am. It just gets better and better!

To know truth is to be set free. Experiencing true love is experiencing true life. To know yourself and be fully known takes perseverance, vulnerability, courage and trust. Don't let pain alienate you from God, but rather let it bond you to Him, to be loved, restored and powerful. Find your voice, share your story and live your essence.

Accepting Jesus's sacrificial love by faith and developing a relationship with Him is the key to receiving love's benefits here in this life and for eternity. If you have never asked Him to come into your heart or if you are concerned about life after death I'd love the privilege to invite you to say this prayer from your heart:

Dear Lord, I realize that I need you in my life and I fall short of your best without your perfect love restoring me.. I ask you come into my heart and live your life through me. I thank you, Jesus, for the terrible price you paid for my sins, but because you did, I now receive your forgiveness and cleansing from the effects of them. Help me to live this day forward in the strength you provide and let my life glorify you. I believe now without a doubt, that I will spend eternity with you, in Jesus name I pray, Amen.

My Prayer for you:

Lord, I pray that all who've taken time to hear about Your goodness in my life would experience You in a new and fresh way. Restore their minds and recover their essence as they read scriptural truths about Your love for them. Open the eyes of their understanding to a love deeper than they've ever known. Help them to surrender every hidden pain and redefine it with the healing power of Your love without shame and to experience your amazing grace at work in them. Guide them to experience a piece of heaven on earth by having great relationships as they experience the freedom to be the person You created them to be. Meanwhile, help them to prepare for Christ's return when we are raptured in oneness with You through the light of Your glory and grace, In Jesus name, Amen.

References

Switch On Your Brain: The Key to Peak Happiness,
Thinking, and Health Sept. 1, 2013
by Caroline Leaf

Broken Children, Grown-Up Pain (Revised): Understanding
the Effects of Your Wounded Past March 10, 2006
by Paul Hegstrom

The Gifts of Imperfection: Let Go of Who You Think You're
Supposed to Be and Embrace Who You Are
September 1, 2010

The Grace Awakening by Charles R. Swindoll, published
by Thomas Nelson (2003) Jan 1, 2003

Disarming the Narcissist: Surviving and Thriving with the
Self-Absorbed 1st (first) Edition by Wendy T. Behary
published by New Harbinger Publications (2008)

Emotional Vampires: Dealing with People Who Drain You
Dry, Revised and Expanded 2nd Edition June 15, 2012
by Albert Bernstein

Becoming Your Own Hero June 27, 2012
by Jordan Paul

Emotional Intelligence 2.0Jun 16, 2009
by Travis Bradberry and Jean Greaves

Having Sex, Wanting Intimacy: Why Women Settle for
One-Sided Relationships Aug 15, 2014
by Jill P. Weber

Dump the Neanderthal; Choose Your Prime Mate
Apr 24, 2012
by Dr. John V. Farrar

Malignant Self-Love: Narcissism Revisited June 30, 2013
by Sam Vaknin and Lidija Rangelovska

Man's Search for Meaning – June 1, 2006
by Viktor E. Frankl

A WOMAN OF SUBSTANCE: Growing Spiritually Mature
in an Immature World -(Unabridged, 8 Volumes in One
Book) July 25, 2012
by Lilliet Garrison

If you would like to find out more about Recovered Essence and access Study Guides or Book Club material, or book Christine to speak at your conference or group, please go to christineawilson.com.

Also you may visit WilsonWellnesCounseling. com to reach Malcolm or Christine Wilson for your counseling, coaching or consulting needs.